LIBERIAN COOKHOUSE COOKING

FOR THE BENEFIT OF
FRIENDS OF LIBERIA

REVISED EDITION

EDITED BY
JOAN KEENAN

Revised edition 2008

Cover art by Roland Svensson
Graphic layout by Joan Keenan and Jean J. Picou

All proceeds from the sale of this book will go to support projects of FRIENDS OF LIBERIA.

For more information, write:
P.O. Box 28098
Washington, D.C. 20016

Library of Congress Control Number: 2008909704
ISBN 978-0-615-25893-5

Printed in the United States of America on recycled paper.

FOR ALL THE CHILDREN OF LIBERIA,
WITH THE HOPE THAT A LASTING PEACE WILL ALLOW
THEM TO PLAY ONCE AGAIN, TO ATTEND SCHOOL, AND
TO GROW INTO RESPONSIBLE LIBERIAN CITIZENS.

Betty Stull Schaffer

CONTENTS

INTRODUCTION

This cookbook was written with a twofold purpose: to introduce the reader to Liberia and its cooking, and to raise money to support the work of the Friends of Liberia. It succeeded in doing both. I made new friends and learned new skills, while feeling that, in a small way, I contributed to the rebuilding of Liberia.

Throughout the process, I was reminded of the similarities between Liberian and the cooking of the Caribbean, where I now live. Of course, when one looks at the tropical climates of both places, one can see that the same basic ingredients are available. Historically there has been the interchange of peoples, Africans brought to America as slaves and African-Americans returning to establish Liberia as a country. Recipes and seeds were carried back and forth. Recipes were adapted to the new environments.

In spite of the similarities, cultural preferences continue to give each style of cooking it's own unique flavor. One major difference seems to be in the use of spices. West Indian cooking depends heavily on "seasoning" thyme, chibble, garlic, etc., while the Liberian main dishes depend mostly on salt, black pepper and Liberian hot, HOT peppers. The second difference would be in the cooking oils used. Many Caribbean islands depend on coconut oil for cooking, while Liberians use palm oil with its distinctive red color and strong flavor.

Many of the recipes given here are not "country chop," but are what is called "Kwi," or town cooking. Most of the country did not have electricity when I was there, refrigerators and frozen foods were not readily available. Cocktail parties were not happening in the countryside where I lived, but were definitely in with the more affluent Liberians. Other recipes were used and enjoyed throughout the country. I have included recipes for which the ingredients are readily available, but a few others were included just to give an idea of traditional Liberian food.

This book exceeded original expectations. Not only did it bring new fans to Liberian cooking, but it fed a network of people committed to helping Liberians, particularly the children. Some of the original contributors, including myself, got involved in a hands-on way, creating a teacher training project that has touched thousands of children's lives and revived teachers' enthusiasm for their vocation. The book continues to help keep that going.

Joan Keenan
EDITOR, 2008

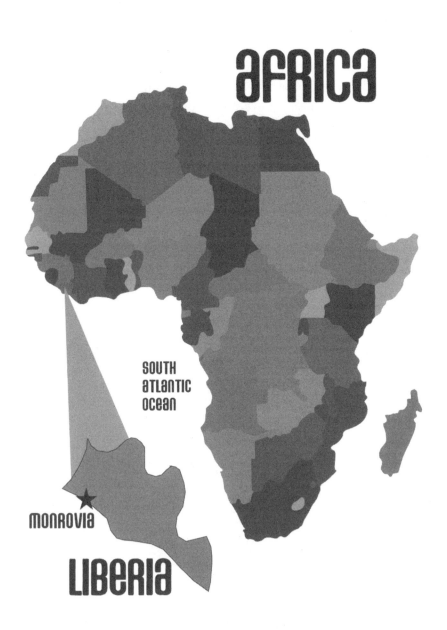

africa

SOUTH
ATLANTIC
OCEAN

MONROVIA

LIBERIA

a BRIEF HISTORY OF LIBERIA

African Americans, many of whom were former slaves, began settling in Liberia in the early 1800s. For some immigrants, the new land represented an opportunity denied to them in the United States, for others it was a move "back to Africa," though not necessarily the part of Africa their ancestors were taken from generations before. Regardless of their reason for setting out, the settlers confronted challenges as harsh as, if not more difficult than any encountered by U.S. pioneers in the Western United States. In 1847, when Liberia became the first country on the continent to declare itself an independent republic, its early leaders were from the American settler community. The indigenous people of Liberia in tribes speaking more than twenty-eight dialects, and with spiritual practices from animism to Islam and across the spectrum of Christianity, were excluded from top positions of power for most of the next century and a half.

Though the 20th century brought universal education, a competitive literacy rate and one of the more prosperous economies in West Africa, full democracy and inclusion for all the peoples of the country were elusive.

In 1980, President William Tolbert was assassinated in a coup that led to four years of military rule by Samuel K. Doe of the Armed Forces of Liberia. A 1985 election that appeared to affirm Doe's rule was generally considered to be fraudulent and civil unrest and spreading political opposition followed. In 1989, a former government minister, Charles Taylor, led an invasion of Liberia from western Ivory Coast that became a catalyst for long-standing political, ethnic, and economic grievances to erupt into full-scale civil war. For more than a decade, the conflict wracked the country with random violence and massacres, destroyed the economy, and claimed at least 200,000 lives. Half the prewar population of two and a half million people was displaced in the country or forced toflee elsewhere. Liberians sought refuge in countries around the world.

This cookbook was originally published in 1997, just after war-weary Liberians elected warlord Taylor to the presidency. Friends of Liberia from around the world, using the newly accessible Internet, contributed recipes and reminiscences, art and artifacts to conjure up a Liberia of memory and express hope for the future. Sale of the cookbook raised thousands of dollars for projects in Liberia to benefit children — rebuilding schools, training teachers and building libraries. Only recently, Liberians have truly been able to hope for a peaceful future. The cookbook will once again contribute to that future with a loving remembrance of the former Liberia and a helping hand for the new Liberia.

PAT REILLY
SECRETARY
FRIENDS OF LIBERIA

Friends of Liberia is a group that is as good as its name. Most of its 800 members have lived and worked in Liberia at some time during the last several decades. We were teachers, farmers, missionaries, fishermen, miners, administrators, journalists, health workers, businessmen, and diplomats during our time in that beautiful place. Since the outbreak of war in 1989, we have brought our collective expertise to the common purpose of ending the civil war and rebuilding the country. For us, this tragedy has a human face; the dead include friends, former neighbors, colleagues, and family members. People we care deeply about have had their lives brutally interrupted, have been displaced and face uncertain futures. A generation of children has known nothing but war and deprivation. Just as knowing Liberians intensifies our sorrow, knowing the potential of Liberians allows us to say with confidence that this nation will rise again to take its place among the leaders of Africa.

A high point of life in Liberia, whether in the rich, quiet rhythms of the village, or the hurly-burly vibrancy of its towns and cities, was always mealtime. The abundant trees, rich vegetation, good soil and expanse of ocean yielded up fruits, vegetables, and tasty fish and meat that would be brought together in "soups," spiked with hot pepper and served on beds of moist, steamy rice.

This book shares with you some of the recipes associated with Liberia and some of the memories the food conjures up for our members. We have also brought together some Liberian proverbs about life, many of them revolving around food. Many of the pictures are from slides taken by Peace Corps Volunteers in the 1960s. Permission to use original artwork has been graciously granted by the artists.

This book honors a happier time, when life in Liberia was "sweet, like chicken soup." And it also welcomes a time when peace will allow Liberia to get back to the gentler pursuits of living.

PaT ReILLY

FOL PROJECTS

When Friends of Liberia (FOL) first published the cookbook, it was rebuilding two elementary schools. The challenges of such bricks and mortar projects, though satisfying in their tangible end product, weren't ideally suited to a small U.S.-based organization. Brought together in the creation of this cookbook, a group of teachers began to wonder what was going on inside Liberian schools. Surveys and research indicated that after a decade of civil war, though schooling was still a Liberian priority, most teachers were not only without books, paper and chalk, but had not had any professional development in a long time or, in many cases, ever.

The Liberian Education Assistance Project (LEAP) brought five annual workshops to Liberia between 1999 and 2004 with volunteer U.S. teachers to teach primary-grade teachers about inter-active, child-centered K-3 learning. Trainees became trainers and brought the concepts back to their communities. The trainers formed a non-profit teacher training organization, incorporated in Liberia, and also called LEAP, but in their case Liberian Educators for Action and Peace. They continue to train others and seek funding to expand their program around the country.

FOL has also funded a libraries project, which teaches schools in Liberia how to maintain libraries and make them relevant.

As Liberia struggles to rebuild itself as a nation, Friends of Liberia will continue to find new ways to support Liberian efforts toward achieving quality universal education.

PAT REILLY

A DIETITIAN'S THOUGHTS ON LIBERIAN FOOD

Before I left for Liberia, a food and nutrition professor in the United States told me I would find the food available to eat offering at best a monotonous menu of soup and rice. Instead I discovered a variety. The way vegetable and protein sources were blended offered many new tasting experiences. I wanted to decrease the hot pepper so I could taste these new flavors. Tribal variations in preparing food added another dimension. For example, hard-boiled eggs in palm butter made by a Grebo woman and rice that was checked with greens were two delights when I visited upcountry .

Rice, although the staple, was not the only starch. I grew to enjoy dumboy, fufu, and eddoes. Once when I was enjoying eddoes, a Liberian advised me that eddoes were poor peoples' food. Perhaps I lost some class distinction in his eyes, but I was intrigued with the idea that even in a poor country, food indicated one's wealth.

I wondered, why so many soup dishes? Why is everything cooked so long? When I looked carefully at the equipment available to heat food, as well as containers to store food during the cooking process, I began to answer my questions. Over time, I grew to enjoy the sociality that occurred with the lengthy food preparation process. I learned to swallow chunks of fufu and dumboy. The day I understood the description of a person, who was not very intelligent, stated as "He probably chews his fufu," I thought, "Perhaps I do know part of what is happening here."

My travels upcountry lead to seeing many people with enlarged goiters. I wondered if it was lack of iodine source or was something interfering with iodine absorption. Mesurado Fish was a growing company throughout the Republic, so I began to encourage consumption of fish and iodized salt. Perhaps this nutritional problem could be prevented. I have since learned that cassava might limit the absorption of iodine.

The amount of carbohydrate and protein combination in the Liberian diet lends well to the USDA Food Pyramid. If the amount of fat were a little more carefully controlled, it would be beneficial. One nutrient of initial concern was calcium. However, discovering that eating of fish bones and chicken bones was acceptable, decreased this concern. Iron was another concern, and the prevalence of anemia confirmed this. It seems that distribution of available food rather than availability of nutritious food was the bigger concern.

So, the byword on Liberian cooking might well be: watch the fats and load up on the greens, and by all means enjoy.

DOROTHY WRASE HARES RD

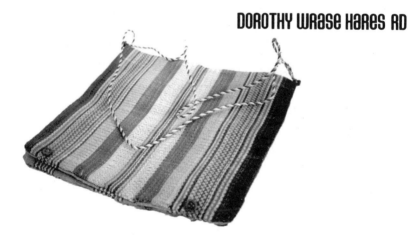

acknowledgments

This book was originally meant to be a small pamphlet to be sold here on St. Croix to raise a few dollars for the Friends of Liberia annual fund-raising effort. I have my friends from Courtyard Players to thank (I think) for encouraging me to make it into a book. I would like to especially thank Marguerite MacKay and Lorraine Joseph for giving me that push to go ahead, when I was sure I could not handle it.

A very special thank you to Pat Reilly. She and I only met after we became e-mail friends. She gave me the encouragement, and practical support to develop my ideas into a book. She was right there, on my computer, ready to make contacts for me, get pictures, proofread, write and rewrite, and help gather information. I couldn't have, wouldn't have, done it without her help.

Thanks to my co-workers at Charles H. Emanuel School and Edith Gordon, a fellow Peace Corps volunteer in Liberia, who helped try out recipes, either baking them or tasting them.

Many of the recipes were taken from The Liberian Way of Cooking, compiled by the International Women's Club of Liberia, Come Let's Eat, by June Grabemeyer, Kwi Style Cooking by Kathy d'Azevedo, Liberian Cook Book by Emily Guegbeh Peal. Others are recipes that I have used and adapted from my Peace Corps experience in Owensgrove, Liberia. Still others were offered by former volunteers and Liberians living in the United States.

Parables were recalled by John Singler, a former Fulbright scholar, and Steve Keenan and John Kucij, former Peace Corps volunteers. Joseph Barchue, a Liberian studying in Alabama, provided the explanation of several Liberian parables plus several recipes. Albert Broplah, now living in Kansas, shared proverbs from a book he used in high school in Liberia.

Thanks to my brother, John Keenan, for spending hours at his computer scanning in my ancient slides. Eristus Mitchell, a young Crucian, produced original pencil sketches of fruits and vegetables just for this book. John Jones, an art teacher and professional artist, created drawings based on my old slides.

Roland Svensson, of Sweden, graciously gave us permission to use his sketches and watercolors of Liberian scenes from the 1960s to compliment the text.

Esther Warner Dendel offered her never before published story, A Spoon is for Stirring, and the wonderful fifty-year-old print of Chief Kondea.

I thank all who were encouraging and supportive. Thanks to my husband, Donatus St. Aimee, for his patience and support, as I became glued to my computer, trying to master the intricacies of desktop publishing, scanning, etc.

And a final thank you to Lucretia Diggs, my friend and "other mother," who was always supportive, and willing to try my recipes. Lucretia passed away before she could see the finished book, but I know she is smiling now.

JOAN KEENAN
EDITOR

BREADS

BREADS

In the interior of the country, shortbreads, biscuits, and cookies would often be cooked in cast-iron dutch ovens over an open fire. A small camp-style oven on top of a kerosene stove was another way of baking. Bread usually was not served with a meal, but was eaten for breakfast or as a snack. Eating habits change, however, as people leave the countryside and move to the city.

Short bread, an old Montserrado County tradition, is usually prepared with bleached flour. Angela Peabody began feeding her family whole wheat short bread a couple of years ago for health purposes.

WHOLE WHEAT SHORT BREAD

3 C. WHOLE WHEAT FLOUR
1/2 C. SUGAR
2 T. BAKING POWDER
1 TSP. SALT
1/2 C. BUTTER OR MARGARINE
1 TSP. NUTMEG
1/3 C. MILK

Combine ingredients in order listed, mixing with a fork each time a new ingredient is added. Add milk slowly, blending it into mixture until moist. Fold into well-greased baking pan and bake at 350°F until browned. May be served hot with butter or even fish gravy.

ANGELA PEABODY

Roland Svensson

EDITOR'S NOTE: *This recipe is a favorite of mine. It tastes like the short bread I used to buy in Owensgrove, Grand Bassa County. I would try to get it when it was hot from the oven and then smear it with strawberry jam. M-m-m!*

SHORT BREAD

2 C. FLOUR
1/2 C. SHORTENING
2/3 C. MILK
4 TSP. BAKING POWDER
1 TSP. SALT
1 EGG (OPTIONAL)
2 T. SUGAR

Sift flour, sugar, baking powder, and salt together. Cut in shortening with fork or pastry blender. Stir in milk until dough is soft and light. Spoon the dough into a greased 9-inch square pan and bake at 350°F until done.

THE LIBERIAN WAY OF COOKING

SHORT BAKING POWDER BISCUITS

2 C. ALL-PURPOSE FLOUR
1/2 C. SHORTENING
1 T. BAKING POWDER
2/3 C. MILK
1/2 TSP. SALT
1 EGG (OPTIONAL)

Sift flour, baking powder, and salt into mixing bowl. Cut in shortening with pastry blender or fork. If desired, beat egg and add to mixture. Using fork, quickly stir in milk. Add more milk if necessary until dough is soft and light, but not sticky. Turn out onto a floured surface. With floured hands, pat down or knead about 20 strokes until smooth. Roll lightly to 1/4-inch thick. Shape with biscuit cutter (drinking glass or tin can) or roll into an oblong and cut into diamonds with a knife. Place on an ungreased cookie sheet (close together for soft biscuits, one inch apart for crusty ones). Prick with a fork. Bake 12 to 15 minutes at 450°F.

THE LIBERIAN WAY OF COOKING

Only those who have teeth worry about toothache.

Louise Siebo sold candies, cakes, and biscuits at Kingville, No. 7. Edith and her housemate, Cecelia, often got them for a snack. Mrs. Seibo gave Edith this recipe to take with her when she was leaving Liberia.

LOUISE SIEBO'S BISCUITS

1 C. SIFTED FLOUR
2 TSP. BAKING POWDER
1/2 TSP. SALT
2 HEAPING TSP. SHORTENING
4 TSP. SUGAR
4 T. MILK
1/4 TSP. NUTMEG OR 1/2 TSP. VANILLA

Mix dry ingredients together and cut in shortening. Then add "small" nutmeg or vanilla (dough should remain soft). Roll out on floured surface, until about 1/4-inch thick. Cut biscuit size, using drinking glass, and place on ungreased cookie sheet. Bake at 350° to 375°F until slightly brown.

EDITH GORDON

You can't carry a bag of salt and look for rain.

MEANING:
You can't put up an argument and defeat your own purpose.

Rice bread is served warm at breakfast with fried or baked fish, or eggs.

angela's modern rice bread

2 C. CREAM OF RICE®
3 T. SUGAR
1/2 TSP. SALT
4 TSP. BAKING POWDER
1/2 TSP. NUTMEG
1-1/2 C. MASHED BANANAS
2 EGGS, BEATEN LIGHTLY
1-1/2 C. EVAPORATED MILK
1 TSP. VANILLA EXTRACT
1 C. OLIVE OIL

Mix dry ingredients. Gradually add bananas, eggs, milk, and vanilla. Add oil and mix thoroughly. Bake in well-greased 8x 12-inch pan at 350°F for about 45 minutes.

angela peabody

LIBERIAN RICE BREAD

2 C. MASHED BANANAS (UNEATABLY RIPE IS BEST!)
2 C. CREAM OF RICE®
1/3 C. SUGAR
4 TSP. BAKING POWDER
1 C. MILK
FEW GRAINS NUTMEG (OPTIONAL)
1/2 TSP. SALT
2/3 C. VEGETABLE OIL

Blend overripe bananas to reach the two cup mark in the
blender. Add remaining ingredients and blend until completely
mixed. Pour into one large or two small greased loaf pans. A
large cast-iron skillet works well also. Bake at 325°F for about
one hour, or until the loaf tests done with a toothpick and the
top is a light golden brown.

KAREN DAHN

If you want to see the belly of an ant, you must take time.

PINEAPPLE NUT BREAD

2-1/2 C. FLOUR
1/2 TSP. SALT
1 T. BAKING POWDER
1/2 TSP. BAKING SODA
1 C. WHOLE BRAN
1 EGG UNBEATEN
3 T. BUTTER OR COOKING OIL
3/4 C. PINEAPPLE (DRAINED)
3/4 C. CHOPPED WALNUTS OR 1/2 C. PEANUTS

Sift dry ingredients together. Stir in remaining ingredients. Mix well. Bake in greased loaf pan at 350°F for about 1-1/4 hours or until knife inserted in middle comes out clean. Keep 14 hours before cutting.

THE LIBERIAN WAY OF COOKING

COCONUT BREAD

1 GRATED COCONUT
2 C. SUGAR
1/2 LB. SOFT BUTTER
3 EGGS
1/2 TSP. ALLSPICE
1 TSP. CINNAMON
1-1/2 TSP. VANILLA
1 C. MILK, MIXED WITH
1/2 C. COCONUT WATER
2 LBS. FLOUR
3 TSP. BAKING POWDER

Mix together in order given and bake in greased loaf pan at 325°F for 1-1/4 hours. Remove from pan at once.

EMILY GUEGBEH PEAL
THE LIBERIAN COOKBOOK

11

CORN BREAD

1 C. BUTTER OR MARGARINE
1 C. SUGAR
1-1/2 C. CORN MEAL
1 C. FLOUR
1/2 TSP. SALT
1 T. BAKING POWDER
1 C. MILK
2 EGGS
DASH NUTMEG

Soften butter and blend in sugar. Gradually add corn meal, salt, flour, and milk. Break eggs into mixture and mix well. Add baking powder and nutmeg last; stir. Pour batter into greased 9-inch square pan. Bake at 350°F for 20-30 minutes. Serve hot. Makes 6 to 8 servings.

THE LIBERIAN WAY OF COOKING

SWEET POTATO BREAD

1 C. FINELY MASHED SWEET POTATOES
1 TSP. SALT
1/2 YEAST CAKE (1 ENVELOPE DRY YEAST)
2 T. WARM WATER
2-3/4 C. FLOUR

Add salt to the potatoes. Dissolve yeast in water, add to potatoes. Mix in enough flour to make a soft sponge. Cover, set aside in a warm place to rise. When light, add the remainder of flour to make a smooth elastic dough. Cover and set aside to rise—about 1 hour. Mold and shape into a loaf or rolls. Let rise again. Bake in moderate oven (350°F) one hour for loaf, 25 to 30 minutes for rolls.

THE LIBERIAN WAY OF COOKING

Eristus Mitchell

14

Banana Bread

1/2 C. SHORTENING OR MARGARINE
1 C. GRANULATED SUGAR
2 EGGS
1 C. BANANAS, MASHED
2 C. FLOUR
3/4 TSP. BAKING POWDER
1/2 TSP. SALT
1/4 C. CHOPPED NUTS
1/4 C. WARM WATER
1 TSP. BAKING SODA

Cream shortening and sugar. Blend in eggs and mashed bananas. Add flour, baking powder, and salt. Mix well. Add nuts. Mix baking soda with warm water, and add to batter. Bake in greased loaf pan at 350°F for 45 to 60 minutes or until knife stuck in center comes out dry. Remove from pan at once.

THE LIBERIAN WAY OF COOKING

Roland Svenson

PLANTAIN GINGERBREAD

1 C. DARK MOLASSES	1/2 TSP. SALT
1/3 C. BUTTER	1-1/2 TSP. BAKING SODA
1/2 C. SUGAR	2 TSP. GINGER
1 C. SOUR MILK	1 TSP. CINNAMON
21/3 C. FLOUR	1/2 TSP. CLOVE
1 TSP. VANILLA	1/4 TSP. NUTMEG
2 LARGE HALF-RIPE PLANTAINS	
(SLICED IN ROUNDS)	

Use a tablespoon of the butter to grease a 9-inch square baking pan. Preheat oven to 350°F. Combine sugar and vanilla in a heavy saucepan with half a cup of water. Add plantain slices and cook over moderate heat until plantains are tender. Drain. Then layer slices across the bottom of the baking dish. Set aside. Combine flour, salt, baking soda, and spices in a bowl. In a clean saucepan, bring butter and molasses just to a boil. Begin adding the flour and spice mixture and the milk, a bit at a time, alternating them. Beat vigorously. When all the remaining ingredients have been added to the pan, and the mixture is smooth, pour over plantains in baking dish. Bake 50 minutes to 1 hour, or until a knife inserted into the center comes out clean.

THE LIBERIAN WAY OF COOKING

If the river did not carry you away, will the creek do so?

MEANING:
If great things do not move you, will smaller ones do so?

Banana Cream of Wheat® Bread

2 C. CREAM OF WHEAT® (NOT INSTANT VARIETY)
1-1/2 C. MASHED BANANAS
1 T. SUGAR
2 EGGS
4 TSP. BAKING POWDER
1/2 C. OIL
1/2 TSP. NUTMEG
1-1/2 C. WATER
1/2 TSP. SALT

Mix dry ingredients. Gradually add bananas, eggs, water and then the oil. Blend thoroughly. Bake at 350°F in a greased 8 x 12-inch pan for 45 minutes or until knife stuck in center comes out clean. Remove from pan and cool on rack.

Emily Guegbeh Peal
LIBERIAN COOKBOOK

PANCAKE WITH EGG, PLEASE!

Sometimes we get just what we ask for! During in-country training in Zwedru, Grand Gedeh county, a few of us decided to splurge for breakfast at the local kwi (Lebanese) restaurant. Besides the usual chop the menu offered:

One egg _____	$1.00
One pancake_____	$ .75
One pancake with egg ____	$1.50

Always searching for the good deal, my friend ordered the pancake with egg. After the usual long wait, probably while an egg was searched for, my friend's plate arrived with only a pancake. He ignorantly stated, "I ordered a pancake with egg!" "That is a pancake with egg," was the reply. "But where's the egg?" pleaded my friend. "It's in the pancake batter, of course," was the answer.

MIKE ROBINSON

PUMPKIN BREAD

1-1/2 C. SUGAR
1/3 C. SHORTENING
2 EGGS
1-2/3 C. FLOUR
1/4 TSP. BAKING POWDER
1 TSP. BAKING SODA
3/4 TSP. SALT
1/2 TSP. CINNAMON
1/4 TSP. GROUND CLOVES
1/3 C. WATER
1 C. MASHED PUMPKIN
1/2 C. CHOPPED NUTS (OPTIONAL)

Preheat oven to 350° F. Grease two 8-inch loaf pans. In mixing bowl, cream sugar and shortening. Add eggs one at a time, beating well after each addition. Stir in dry ingredients. Stir in water, pumpkin, and nuts. Pour batter into pans. Bake for 1 hour.

COME LETS EAT

Roland Svensson

21

Palm Wine

Raphia vinifera is an important palm tree in Liberia since it serves as the source of palm wine, an alcoholic beverage enjoyed by many Liberians. It is served at feasts and is offered to honored guests. Drinking it can take on symbolic importance, as the sharing of palm wine can be used to repair social relationships.

The tree is found growing near rivers and streams. When a young man finds a tree, it is considered his for life. In order to tap the tree, a small hole is drilled through the bark and wood near the top, and a tube is inserted. The sap is forced out through the tube and collected in a gourd or other container. Several pints of foamy sap can be collected each day. Since the sap is rich in sugar, it will quickly ferment if left standing. This produces a slightly fizzy alcoholic drink. The longer it is allowed to ferment, the stronger and more sour it becomes.

While palm wine is not readily available to us, I am sure some of you would like to experiment using other alcoholic beverages to see how this bread turns out.

First taste the palm wine before you say you will never drink it.

MEANING:
If you have not tried something out, you will not know what it is like.

PALM WINE BREAD

2 LB. FLOUR
3/4 PT. WARM WATER
2 OZ. SUGAR
1/2 PT. PALM WINE
1 TSP. SALT

Dissolve sugar in palm wine. In separate bowl, sift flour and salt. Combine liquid and flour, and mix to a soft elastic dough. Knead on a floured board until smooth. Place in a floured bowl, cover with damp cloth and put in a warm place to rise until it has doubled its bulk. Knead again lightly on a floured board. Cut into desired shapes. Put large loaves in pans and force down well into corners. Allow to rise again for about 15 minutes. Bake in a hot oven (425°F) for about 15 minutes, then at 375°F until done. Cool on a wire tray or across tops of pans.

THE LIBERIAN WAY OF COOKING

Roland Svenson

CASSAVA BREAD

1/2 C. GRANULATED SUGAR
1/4 LB. BUTTER OR MARGARINE
1 C. GRATED FRESH COCONUT
1-1/2 C. GRATED FRESH CASSAVA
1/2 TSP. BAKING SODA
1 TSP. VANILLA
1/2 C. EVAPORATED MILK

Blend butter and sugar. Add grated coconut, cassava and baking soda. Add evaporated milk and vanilla, mix well and pour into well-greased loaf pan. Bake at 300°F one hour or until almost done. Increase temperature to 375°F during last minutes to brown. Remove from pan. Serve hot or cold. Fine with coffee or tea.

THE LIBERIAN WAY OF COOKING

24

NOTE: *You may line a greased pan with banana leaves (if available). Grease leaves. Saves washing a crusty pan!*

CASSAVA COCONUT BARS

1/2 C. SUGAR
1/2 C. BUTTER OR MARGARINE
1 C. GRATED FRESH COCONUT
1-1/2 C. GRATED FRESH CASSAVA
1/2 TSP. SALT
1/2 TSP. BAKING SODA
1 TSP. VANILLA
1/2 C. EVAPORATED MILK
2 EGGS
1 C. RAISINS

Blend butter and sugar. Add grated coconut and cassava. Beat eggs and add to the batter with the remaining ingredients. Pour into well-greased loaf pan. Bake at 300°F for 1 hour. Increase heat to 375°F for the last 5 to 8 minutes to brown. Remove from pan. Serve hot or cold. If cassava is old (dry), use more milk. If cassava is very young, decrease milk.

MILLY BAKER
PHEBE COOKBOOK

main Dishes

main DISHES

a SPOON IS FOR STIRRING
a STORY BY eSTHeR WaRNeR DeNDeL

In the long ago time when God first made people, those people did not know how to do anything. God had to live with them and show them. He slept in a hammock in the palaver house. One thing at a time, he taught them what they needed to know. They learned how to make bowls out of clay and how to make a fire to cook their food. They learned to grow rice and the women learned how to beat it in a mortar to loosen the hulls on the grain. The carver learned how to carve spoons out of wood. A stick from the bush is no good for stirring what you cook. You need a spoon.

One thing God had no need to show these people. They knew how to be hungry. They were hungry all the time. Until they were ready to learn the proper way to cook and eat, God just told them to eat bananas and soursop and wild mushrooms and pineapples.

When God was ready to teach them about eating he had them sit in a circle around a big wooden bowl. He sat with them. The bowl was filled with rice he had showed them how to cook. It was mixed with ground peas (peanuts) that had been beaten in a mortar and roasted in the fire. Each little grain of rice was coated with mashed ground pea. All the food was hot, evenly hot, because it had been stirred with the big spoon the carver had made.

God sent everyone to wash his hands. When they were seated again in a circle each was told to place his clean right hand in the big bowl and pick up a small, small amount of food. He was to roll it into a little ball and then pop it into his mouth. After that, he was to chew, chew, chew before he swallowed.

All but one person did as he was told. That one man, Bo was his name, looked at the big stirring spoon. It gave him an idea. He saw that he could make a big, big ball of rice if he picked it up with the spoon instead of his fingers. That is just what he did.

God was vexed when he saw what the man had done, plenty vexed. When God cooled down small from the heat of his vex he told the man about punishment. The man must sit alone when he ate. For one whole moon, the man must sit alone.

"When you sit all alone eating with a spoon," God said, "what you eat will have no taste. All you will feed is your belly. The fault is not in the spoon. The fault is in eating alone."

OLD KONDEA, THE WOODCARVER
Esther Warner Dendel

THE "AMERICAN" SPOON

A Spoon Is For Stirring is a Bassa story told to me in Liberia by my beloved friend and carving teacher, Chief Kondea. He carved rice bowls and spoons for each of my regular guests at table and adjusted the size of each by whatever I told him about the habits of the friend. One day Kondea brought me a gift which he said was an American spoon. I told him it was beautiful but that I did not know why it was "American." It had been carved out of wild rubber wood and was about a foot long. The center section was round and could easily be curled about with the thumb and fingers. There was a bowl at each end. Regardless of how one grasped the center section, one bowl was turned up and the other down.

Kondea then showed me that while scooping up food with the "up" bowl one could quickly give a twist of the wrist and as soon as one had the contents of the first bowl in his mouth he could be scooping up the next bite with the other bowl. The "American spoon" was his silent comment on the eating habits of my friends.

ESTHER WARNER DENDEL

33

Roland Svenson

GOAT SOUP

3 OR 4 LB. GOAT MEAT
4 MEDIUM ONIONS
6 FRESH TOMATOES
HOT PEPPERS TO TASTE
3 QT. WATER
2 T. TOMATO PASTE
SALT AND BLACK PEPPER
STOCK FISH AND BONNIES
(DRIED FISH) MAY BE ADDED

Cut goat meat into cubes about 2 inches square. Wash and season with salt, black pepper and hot peppers. Cover with sliced onions. Let stand for 60 minutes to allow seasoning to soak in. Add 3-4 quarts of water and boil until meat is tender. Add remaining onions, fresh tomatoes, and tomato paste. More water may be added if desired. Continue cooking until meat is tender, and tomato is soft. Serve hot.

THE LIBERIAN WAY OF COOKING

Peace Corps Peppers

My wife Lois and I were Peace Corps Volunteers in Tappita with the first group of volunteers to serve in Liberia. The original seeds came from a bush growing behind our house. In 1962, we sent some pepper seeds home to Lois' mother, who grew them in Ohio. On our return, we shared seeds with our friends, Dave and Alice Chung Phillips, who grew them for a few years in a tiny Chinese kitchen garden. During the middle 1970s we were still propagating the peppers ourselves on the floor of Havasu Canyon, until a horse got into our yard one night and ate our only bush. I always thought this must have caused one surprised horse! We were grief stricken until we learned that the Phillipses still had six seeds left in an envelope.

As the seeds had lain dormant for so many years, we were not optimistic, but we planted them and waited. And waited. Only ONE finally germinated. We babied that cutie along for months, hand pollinating the blossoms with Q-tips as they appeared.

When the first Liberian Peace accord was signed, we offered to send seeds to members of the Friends of Liberia newsgroup on the nascent replacement for the village drum, the Internet. We have sent out seeds to at least thirty people and as far away as the Ukraine. Several people have been so gracious as to share palm oil and palm oil soup with us. And, if the peace holds, it will all surpass our wildest dreams.

STEVE HIRST

Betty Stull Schaffer

GROUNDNUT (PEANUT) SOUP

2 LB. MEAT OR CHICKEN
1/2 C. OIL
1 C. WHOLE TOMATOES, MASHED
1 MEDIUM ONION, CHOPPED
1 C. PEANUT BUTTER (UNSWEETENED)
2 C. WATER
SALT AND HOT PEPPER TO TASTE

Cut meat or chicken into chunks. Brown in oil. Heat and remove remaining oil in sauce pan and add tomatoes, onion, pepper, and salt. Simmer 15 minutes. Add browned meat. Dilute peanut butter with water, add to meat mixture, and mix well. Cover and cook until meat is tender, about 20-40 minutes. Serve over rice.

COME LET'S EAT

CHICKEN DINNER

On a visit to my friend Ahmed's uncle, we were given a small white chicken. Ahmed proudly carried it home under his arm over four hours of bush trails. When we reached our village, Ahmed built a small wire enclosure to hold this chicken until it would be time to cook it. The time came sooner than we had planned. The next morning, I woke up to driver ants everywhere. I looked for our white chicken and saw only a black ball. The ants had completely covered it and killed it. It hadn't been able to run away. Ahmed came running to my screams. He picked up the chicken, beat it against the wall, put it in boiling water, and then plucked it. We cooked it for dinner that night.

SALLY GOSLINE HUMPHREY

*If a chicken with a lot of feathers can feel cold,
how much more can featherless chickens?*

MEANING:
If he who has, can get jam, what about he who has nothing?

CHICKEN SOUP

1 MEDIUM-SIZE CHICKEN, CUT UP
2 MEDIUM ONIONS, SLICED
2 T. TOMATO PASTE
2 GREEN PEPPERS, SLICED
2 PODS HOT PEPPERS (OPTIONAL)
SALT AND BLACK PEPPER TO TASTE
3 QT. WATER
2 WHITE POTATOES

Season chicken well. Let stand to allow seasoning to go through. Add water and onions and bring to a boil. Add other ingredients and let cook slowly until chicken is tender. Serve hot. Serves 6 - 8. This soup is highly recommended for sick people.

THE LIBERIAN WAY OF COOKING

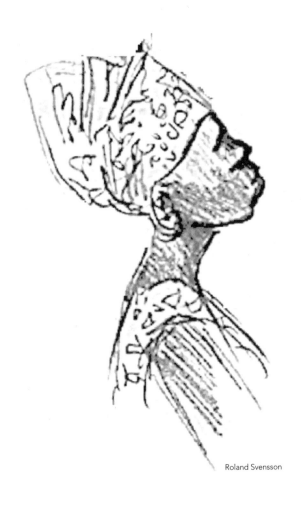

Roland Svensson

40

cassava soup

2 LARGE CASSAVA, DICED
1 MEDIUM ONION, MINCED
2 C. MILK
1-1/2 T. BUTTER
SALT, PEPPER, CELERY SALT,
OR CHOPPED CELERY
ANISEED TO TASTE (OPTIONAL)

Peel and dice cassava. Cook in small amount of water until tender. The water should be cooked down so there is little left. To the cassava and remaining liquid, add minced onion, salt, pepper, celery salt (or chopped celery) and milk. Simmer five minutes. Add aniseed in soup (optional). Just before serving, add butter. Serve with soft-boiled eggs.

THE LIBERIAN WAY OF COOKING

PUMPKIN SOUP

1 LARGE BUTTERNUT SQUASH
1 ONION
2 FRESH JALAPENO PEPPERS
1/2 TSP. SALT
1 BOUILLON CUBE
1 CLOVE GARLIC
2 LB. STEW MEAT OR CHICKEN
1-1/2 C. WATER
3 T. COOKING OIL.

Cut butternut squash into small cubes (1 sq. cm). Cut up onion and fresh jalapeno as small as possible, and mince the garlic. The meat should be cubed as well. Braise the meat with garlic and pepper in oil and set aside while you boil the remaining ingredients in a covered pot. Once the squash becomes tender, add the meat/oil mixture and continue cooking with cover off until the water has all but evaporated. Stir periodically. If you want to get fancy, add some peppercorns toward the end of the cooking. Serve with your favorite rice. Enjoy!

CARL DEALY

42

PHEBE PUMPKIN SOUP

1 LB. MEAT
1 C. VEGETABLE OIL
2-3 C. DICED PUMPKIN
2 BOUILLON CUBES
1 CHOPPED ONION
SALT AND PEPPER
WATER

Cut meat into small pieces and season with salt and pepper. Allow to stand 30 minutes. Fry meat in 1/4 cup oil until well browned. Add water to cover and cook until tender. In another pan, fry diced pumpkin and onion in remaining oil. Cover and cook on medium fire for 10 minutes stirring often. Add broth from meat and bouillon (if canned meat is used, add 1 cup water). Cook 10 minutes covered. Add meat and hot pepper if desired. Cook uncovered until the water has been absorbed and only oil remains. Add salt and pepper if needed. Serve on hot rice.

NANCY SWINGLE
PHEBE COOKBOOK

NOTE: *Check dried codfish for saltiness. If very salty it may need to be soaked overnight. You may be able to eliminate adding salt.*

Beef Internal Soup

1 LB. STEW BEEF, CUT IN 1/2-INCH CUBES
1/2 LB. TRIPE, CUT IN SMALL PIECES
1 CAN TOMATO PASTE (6 OZ.)
1 TSP. SALT
1 TSP. COARSE RED PEPPER
1 TSP. BLACK PEPPER
1/2 LB. FRESH TOMATOES,
CUT IN 1/2-INCH SQUARES
3 QT. WATER
1/2 LB. ONIONS, THINLY SLICED
1/2 LB. DRIED CODFISH, CUT IN SMALL PIECES
1 LARGE SMOKED FISH (HERRING, MACKEREL, WHITEFISH, ETC.)

In a 1-gallon pot, add first seven ingredients to one quart of water. Simmer for one hour or until meat is tender. In another 1-gallon pot, add onions and dried codfish to 2 quarts of water and simmer until fish is tender. Combine fish and meat, and simmer slowly for 2 minutes. Debone the smoked fish and add to soup. Cook about 10 minutes longer. Add more seasoning if necessary. Serve with rice or fufu.

The African Cookbook

SWEET POTATO SOUP

5 C. CHOPPED SWEET POTATO
2-3 LB. CHICKEN OR
1-1/2 LB. FISH
1/3 C. RED PALM OIL
1 MEDIUM ONION, CHOPPED
HOT PEPPER TO TASTE
1 TSP. CHOPPED GARLIC
1 SMALL CAN TOMATO PASTE
1 BOUILLON CUBE
WATER

Sauté chicken or fish in red oil. Add chopped onions, pepper, and garlic. Add diced sweet potatoes (chopped into 1-inch pieces), tomato paste, bouillon cube (dissolved in about a cup of water) and enough water to cover. Cook over medium heat until sweet potatoes are soft and most of the water has been absorbed. Serve with rice.

LAURIE FUNK

SWEET POTATO GREENS?

I live in Western Massachusetts where there are tons of sweet potato farmers. Most sweet potato farmers I've met are all too happy to give me their greens for free. Of course, I've heard the occasional, "You wanna eat the stuff I usually feed the pigs?!" But, I've managed to find a couple who happily call me when they have greens.

After I went back to a farm to ask a second time, the family couldn't believe I was really eating them. So, I cooked some up that night and took them the soup (and rice, of course) the next day. They loved it.

I'm fortunate that I'm able to get the right kind of peppers, as well as palm oil almost year-round. I usually use at least a teaspoon of palm oil, because for me, the soup has to turn your rice orange!

SHEREE MORGAN

46

SWEET POTATO GREENS

4 BUNCHES POTATO GREENS
2 ONIONS
1 C. COOKING OIL
2 PODS HOT PEPPER
3 BONNIES (DRIED FISH)
1 LARGE DRIED FISH
2 PIG'S FEET OR 1/2 LB. HAM

Stem and wash greens two or three times. Cut very fine. Put in pan and wash while rubbing several times until slime is removed. Boil pig's feet until tender to remove salt. Combine greens and onions in hot oil. Fry until greens become wilted. Add fish, boiled pig's feet (or ham) and enough diluted stock from pig's feet to cover. Cook until all water is removed. Serve over rice or cassava.

THE LIBERIAN WAY OF COOKING

CAUTION: *Greens burn easily and stick to bottom of pot. Adjusting the heat and stirring can prevent this.*

JOSEPH'S POTATO GREENS

1 LB. SWEET POTATO GREENS
1 MEDIUM ONION
1/2 TSP. SALT OR
1 BOUILLON CUBE
1/2 TSP. BLACK PEPPER
WHOLE FRESH HOT PEPPER, TO TASTE
1/2 LB. FRESH FISH OR SHRIMP
1/2 LB. BEEF OR CHICKEN
1/2 C. PALM OIL OR VEGETABLE OIL

Wash leaves thoroughly and cut away end of stalks to get rid of rough edges. Shred greens into fine pieces (1-2 mm). There are three ways of doing this:

1) *traditional—hold with hand and slice carefully,*
2) *greens are squeezed, wrung, twisted and rubbed in both hands, or,*
3) *shred in a food processor (the easy way!)*

Cover cut greens with water and wash gently. Gather greens in a ball, squeeze water out gently and place in another dish. Discard water. Cut half of onion on top of greens. Add salt or powdered bouillon cube, black pepper and hot peppers.

Eristus Mitchell

This recipe usually uses a combination of fish or shrimp, with chicken or meat, to enhance the flavor. You can mix and match to suit your taste. Cut the meat/fish combination into bitesize pieces. Season with remainder of cut onion and 1/2 teaspoon salt. Fry meat/fish in hot oil until brown. Remove and place in a dish. Add about 1/3 cup of the oil into a saucepan and heat. Test oil by dropping a tiny piece of onion in it. The onion crackles when oil is ready. Add onions to hot oil, then greens, and stir. Lower heat and cover pan to steam greens. Stir occasionally, cooking for 4 to 5 minutes. Add meat/fish combination and stir in 1/3 cup water. Cook for 10 minutes over medium heat, stirring occasionally. Taste and add more salt if needed.

JOSEPH BARCHUE

49

Photo by: Vertez Burks

JOAN'S LIBERIAN COLLARD GREENS

4 LB. COLLARDS
1 MEDIUM ONION
1 C. COOKING OIL
3 LB. CHICKEN THIGHS
2 T. TOMATO PASTE
2 C. WATER
SALT & BLACK PEPPER (TO TASTE)
HOT PEPPER (TO TASTE)

Wash greens, then chop into 1/4-inch wide pieces. Preheat oil in a large pot. Brown chicken and remove to simmer in its own juices in another pan. Sauté onion until clear, then add collards. Cook for about 5 minutes. Add 2 cups of water, tomato paste, salt, and pepper to taste. Boil for about five minutes, then return chicken and juices to the pot. Continue simmering until tender, about 20 more minutes. Add more water if necessary. Serve over rice.

JOAN KEENAN

CASSAVA LEAF SOUP

3 BUNCHES CASSAVA LEAVES
1 LARGE ONION, SLICED
1 LB. BEEF BRISKET, OR ENTRAILS
2 DRIED FISH, SCALED AND BONED
1/2 DOZ. SHRIMP (OPTIONAL)
SALT TO TASTE
3 BOUILLON CUBES
2-1/2 QT. WATER
1 PT. PALM OIL

Boil meat and dried fish in water with about 2 teaspoons salt.
Pick cassava leaves from stems. (Should be 2-3 cups of leaves.)
Wash thoroughly and drain. Put through grinder with onion, or
beat in mortar until of ground consistency. When meat and fish
are almost done, add shrimp and season soup to taste. Add
bouillon cubes and cassava leaves. Cook over medium heat until
all liquid dries. Add about 1 pint of raw palm oil. Cook about
5 minutes more over low heat. Serve over piping hot rice. Serves
4-6.

FLORENCE WALKER
PHEBE COOKBOOK

CRAWFISH (SHRIMP) BALLS

1 C. GROUND CRAWFISH
1/4 C. CHOPPED ONIONS
1 BOUILLION CUBE
2 T. BREAD CRUMBS
1 EGG
DASH TO TASTE OF :
CHOPPED PARSLEY
BLACK PEPPER
GARLIC SALT
PAPRIKA
HOT PEPPER, FINELY CHOPPED

Combine all ingredients, using half of egg, and shape into balls. Baste balls with other half of egg. Sprinkle with flour and fry until brown.

Gravy for crawfish balls:

1 T. FLOUR
1 T. OIL (USED ABOVE)
2 SLICES ONION
1/2 C. WATER
1 TSP. TOMATO PASTE
SALT, BLACK PEPPER, AND HOT PEPPER TO TASTE

Brown flour in oil. Add tomato paste, onion, salt, black pepper, and hot pepper. Add water and bring to a boil. Put in balls and allow to cook until a gravy consistency is reached.

THE LIBERIAN WAY OF COOKING

52

Anything that is eaten is not wasted.

MEANING:
Any kindness one does has some reward.

Palaver Sauce

2 LB. STEW BEEF, CUT IN 1/2-INCH CUBES
2 QT. WATER
1 T. SALT
4 C. COLLARD GREENS, CHOPPED FINELY
2 C. SPINACH, CHOPPED FINELY
1 LB. BONED SMOKED FISH
1 C. ONION, CHOPPED FINELY
1/2 C. VEGETABLE OR PEANUT OIL
HOT PEPPER TO TASTE

In a one-gallon pot, simmer beef in salted water until half cooked. Add collard greens and spinach and simmer until meat and greens are cooked, about 15 minutes. Add fish and cook for five more minutes, or until all water is absorbed. Sauté onions and hot peppers lightly in a small frying pan, and add to meat mixture. Simmer five minutes longer. Serve with white rice.

THE AFRICAN COOKBOOK

FISH WITH SPICY SAUCE

6 FILLETS OF FRESH MACKEREL, HERRING, OR SIMILAR FISH
2 TSP. SALT
1/2 TSP. BLACK PEPPER
1/2 C. FLOUR
1/2 C. OIL
1 LB. TOMATOES, CHOPPED
1/2 TSP. NUTMEG
1 TSP. CAYENNE PEPPER
2 MEDIUM ONIONS, CHOPPED
PARSLEY, CHOPPED

Wash and dry the fish. Season with salt and black pepper. Coat with flour. Sauté onions in 2 tablespoons oil until clear. Add tomatoes and cayenne. Cook over low heat for 20 minutes. Stir in the nutmeg and salt to taste.

While the sauce is cooking, prepare the fish: Heat the remaining oil in a skillet until it bubbles. Arrange fish in skillet in a single layer and fry until brown on both sides. Drain and arrange on a hot serving dish. Pour sauce over the fish and sprinkle with parsley.

THE LIBERIAN WAY OF COOKING

55

FRESH FISH IN COCONUT CREAM

3 C. COCONUT MILK
1 LB. ONIONS, SLICED THIN
1 TSP. SALT
1/2 TSP. BLACK PEPPER
1 TSP. HOT PEPPER
4 WHOLE FRESH FISH
(ABOUT 1 LB. EACH),
4 OZ. BUTTER

Clean fish and remove heads. Cut fish in half and season with salt and pepper. Sauté onions in butter until soft, but not brown. Add hot pepper. Sauté fish in butter mixture for about 1 minute on each side. Pour coconut milk over fish, cover tightly and simmer gently for 10 minutes. Remove cover and baste constantly until fish is done and sauce has thickened to a creamy consistency (about 10 minutes). Lay fish out on platter with a spatula and pour the sauce over it. Serve with fufu.

MRS. DUKULY
THE AFRICAN COOKBOOK

*A small child should not put his fishing basket
where his hand cannot reach.*

MEANING:
Do not undertake what you cannot accomplish.

SMOKED FISH WITH GRAVY

2 SMOKED FISH
1 ONION, SLICED
1 OR 2 PODS HOT PEPPER, SLICED
2 TSP. FLOUR
1 TSP. TOMATO PASTE
1/2 C. OIL
BLACK PEPPER
1/2 C. WATER

Cut smoked fish into small pieces. Remove all bones and wash several times to remove salt. Fry in hot oil for 5 minutes. Add onion and hot pepper. Fry for another 5 minutes. Add flour and stir until brown. Add tomato paste and mix well. Pour in about 1/2 cup water. Season with black pepper and salt if needed. Cover and cook slowly for 10 minutes. Serve with boiled rice, cassava, or eddoes.

THE LIBERIAN WAY OF COOKING

STEWED FISH

4 FISH STEAKS OR WHOLE FISH
2 T. FLOUR
2 MEDIUM ONIONS, SLICED
4 CARROTS, CUT UP
2 TSP. TOMATO PASTE
1/2 C. COOKING OIL
2 PODS PEPPER, OPTIONAL
SALT AND BLACK PEPPER
1 C. WATER

Season fish with salt and black pepper; dip in flour. Heat oil in saucepan and add fish. Brown lightly. Remove fish and add onions, carrots, and hot pepper to oil. When onions and pepper become slightly cooked, put in remaining flour and stir. Add tomato paste and one cup of water. Stir until sauce begins to thicken. Put fish in sauce, cover pan, and simmer until fish is done.

THE LIBERIAN WAY OF COOKING

STEWED CRAWFISH

AFRICAN MASK - BAOULÉ

LIBERIA 5c

2 LB. CRAWFISH
2 ONIONS
2 GREEN PEPPERS
3 TSP. TOMATO PASTE
3 T. FLOUR
1/2 C. COOKING OIL
SALT AND PEPPER
1 C. WATER

Shell and devein crawfish; wash and season with salt and pepper. Dust with flour and add to hot oil. Fry until slightly cooked; add sliced onions, sliced green peppers, and tomato paste. Mix well and pour in enough water to cover crawfish. Add more seasoning if needed. Cover pot and cook slowly for about 20 minutes.

NOTE: *Shrimp may be substituted for Crawfish*

THE LIBERIAN WAY OF COOKING

59

Photo by: Mary Moran

PALM BUTTER

Palm butter is made from palm nuts, the bright red and yellowish fruit of the palm tree, elaeis guineensis. The nuts are washed and boiled until the skin comes loose from the kernels. The kernels are removed and the rest is put in a mortar and beaten well to form a pulp. This pulp is placed in a pot with enough cold water to cover it. This liquid is then put through a sieve to remove all the fibers and kernels. What comes through is palm butter. It can be cooked with meat or fish, onions, pepper, and salt. It is cooked until it gets thick and then served over rice.

Palm butter is processed and canned in West Africa and can be bought in many ethnic food specialty shops.

JOSEPH'S PALM BUTTER

1/2 LB. MEAT
1 CAN PREPARED PALM PULP
(ABOUT 3-1/2 C.)
1 BOUILLON CUBE
1/2 TSP. BLACK PEPPER
1 OR 2 PODS OF HOT PEPPER
1 MEDIUM ONION, CHOPPED

While smoked meat is usually used in Liberia, fresh meat may be substituted. Cut meat into bitesized pieces and season with chopped onions and black pepper. Steam meat with onion in 1/4 cup water for 5 minutes. Stir in palm pulp and rinse can with 1/3 cup of water and add to stew. Add bouillon cube and hot pepper pods. Cook over medium heat in an uncovered sauce pan for 10-12 minutes. Stir and adjust seasonings to taste. Simmer on very low heat until mixture condenses to a thick sauce. Serve with rice.

CAUTION: *Palm butter splatters. Use deep cooking pot and cover with splatter shield. Putting on the cover is not recommended. It waters down taste and consistency.*

JOSEPH BARCHUE

Mother hen likes the rice fanner with the hole in it.

PLAIN PALM BUTTER

8 C. PALM BUTTER
3 LBS. CHICKEN THIGHS
2 LBS. STEW BEEF, CUT UP
1 LARGE ONION
SALT AND PEPPER TO TASTE
LIBERIAN HOT PEPPER (OPTIONAL)

Season chicken and beef about one hour before cooking. Pour palm butter into a large sauce pan and add chicken, beef, and onion. Add salt, black pepper, and hot pepper to taste. Cook uncovered over a medium flame until it thickens. This takes about one hour. Serve over cooked rice.

THE LIBERIAN WAY OF COOKING

NOTE: *Palm Butter is originally from Cape Palmas in Maryland County, Liberia. However, its aromatic taste has always been enjoyed throughout the country.*

angela's vegetarian palm butter

1 CAN PREPARED PALM PULP (ABOUT 31/2 C.)
FLOWERETTES FROM A MEDIUM-SIZE HEAD OF BROCCOLI
1 C. CUT MUSHROOM
1 C. TOFU, CUT INTO PIECES
2 PODS JALEPENO PEPPER, WHOLE
11/2 TSP. BAY LEAVES
2 C. WATER

Steam broccoli flowerettes, mushroom and jalepeño pepper in water. Add palm butter, tofu, bay leaves, and the following spices:

1/4 TSP. GROUND BLACK PEPPER
1/2 TSP. SALT, OR SALT SUBSTITUTE
1/4 TSP. GARLIC POWDER
1 VEGETABLE BOUILLON CUBE

Let ingredients simmer over low heat until mixture condenses to a thick sauce (about 40 minutes). Serve over rice.

angela peabody

EDITOR'S NOTE: *In Liberia, when I was there, beef was called cow meat. It was hung in the market and pieces were cut off to make the weight desired. It was not sold by cut, and could often take two or more hours to cook before becoming tender enough to chew!*

LIBERIAN BEEF STEW

1 LB. COW MEAT (BEEF)
1 MEDIUM ONION, CHOPPED
3 EDDOES, DICED
3 MEDIUM EGGPLANT, SLICED
1 C. GREEN BEANS (OPTIONAL)
1 CAN WHOLE TOMATOES
SALT, PEPPER, AND HOT PEPPER
2 T. OIL

Cut cow meat into small chunks. Brown beef and chopped onion in oil. Add salt, pepper, and hot pepper to taste. Mix together other ingredients and add to meat and onions. Add enough water to fill pot about 3/4 full, but not covering mixture. Cook until tender.

THE LIBERIAN WAY OF COOKING

Joan Keenan

CANNED CORNED BEEF GRAVY

1 CAN CORNED BEEF
2 T. COOKING OIL
1 T. TOMATO PASTE
1 CAN CORN
1 LARGE ONION
1/2 CUP WATER
HOT PEPPER TO TASTE

Sauté onion and hot pepper in cooking oil. Add corned beef. Mix tomato paste in water and add. Then add canned corn and seasoning. Simmer. Serve over rice.

THE LIBERIAN WAY OF COOKING

A short man does not measure himself in deep water.

FRIED OKRA

2 LBS. FRESH OKRA
1/2 LB. BEEF (CUBED)
1 ONION
1 GREEN PEPPER
1 C. COOKING OIL
1 TSP. TOMATO PASTE
1 C. WATER
SALT AND PEPPER TO TASTE

Brown meat in oil. If meat is not tender, cook longer, so okra does not overcook. (I prefer to use a tender cut of beef like round steak.) Slice okra, onion and pepper and add to the fried meat. Stir and fry until okra slime disappears. Mix tomato paste in water and add to pan. Simmer for about 3-5 minutes. Do not overcook. Serve over cooked rice.

JOAN KEENAN

Roland Svensson

BREADFRUIT STEW

1/2 MEDIUM BREADFRUIT
2 ONIONS
1/4 LB. BUTTER OR MARGERINE
1 LB. SMOKED HAM
SALT AND BLACK PEPPER
TO TASTE
2 QT. WATER

Peel breadfruit and dice. Boil ham in 1 quart of water until tender. Put in breadfruit, sliced onions, and seasoning. Add water to cover. Cook slowly until breadfruit is soft and mushy. More water may be added if needed. Add butter and let simmer for a few minutes. Serve hot.

THE LIBERIAN WAY OF COOKING

67

One tooth cannot make a mouth.

MEANING:
Where there is unity, there is strength.

STEWED EGGPLANT

6 MEDIUM EGGPLANTS
1 ONION
1/2 C. VEGETABLE OIL
4 PIECES FRIED FISH
1/2 LB. BACON OR HAM
2-1/2 C. WATER
SALT AND PEPPER TO TASTE

Slice eggplant very thin. Add oil to pot and saute bacon, onion, and fried fish. Pour in water and add eggplant. Cook for 40 minutes over low flame until eggplant is very soft and mixture has the consistency of stew.

THE LIBERIAN WAY OF COOKING

Photo by: Joan Keenan

eDDOe STEW

4 MEDIUM EDDOES, CUT UP
1/2 LB. SALT PORK OR SALT BEEF
1 SMALL ONION
4 C. WATER
BLACK PEPPER

To remove salt, boil meat in 2 cups of water until almost tender. Drain meat, saving half of stock. To this stock, add 4 cups of water, meat, onions, eddoes, and pepper. Cook until mixture thickens. Serve as a one dish meal with a salad.

VARIATION: *Add 1/2 cup palm oil when combining ingredients.*

THE LIBERIAN WAY OF COOKING

NOTE: *These ingredients are approximate and people should adjust to taste. Liberians, of course, use a lot of hot pepper.*

EGGPLANT CHOP

2 LARGE EGGPLANTS,
PEELED AND CUT INTO CHUNKS
2 LARGE ONIONS, PEELED AND CHOPPED
1 LARGE GREEN PEPPER, DICED
HOT PEPPER AND SALT TO TASTE
2 CANS OF TOMATO SAUCE (16 OZ.)
1/2 C. OIL
1 LB. MEAT, IN SMALL CUBES (OPTIONAL)

Boil eggplant chunks until tender. Drain well and mash to the consistency of applesauce. Put enough oil in pan to sauté onions, green pepper, hot pepper, and meat. Simmer a few minutes more. Add tomato sauce and cook, stirring every so often, until meat is tender. Do not let burn. Serve over cooked rice.

CAROL AND DON HEGMAN

PERLEaU RICE

1 CHICKEN, 3 TO 4 LB.
1 T. SALT
3 TSP. BLACK PEPPER
1/4 C. FLOUR
1/2 C. PALM OIL
1/2 LB. HAM, CUBED
3 QT. WATER
1 LARGE ONION, SLICED
1/3 C. TOMATO PASTE
1/2 C. CHOPPED CABBAGE
2-1/2 C. BROWN RICE
HOT PEPPER TO TASTE

Cut chicken into serving pieces. Wash, drain, and dry. Season with salt and pepper and let stand 15 minutes. Then sprinkle with flour. Heat oil in a heavy pan. Brown chicken in oil lightly on both sides. Remove chicken and place in large pot. Fry ham in remaining oil. Add to chicken. Add water, onion, tomato paste, and cabbage. Cover and simmer until chicken is done, about 20 minutes. Remove chicken from stock and add uncooked rice. Cover and cook for 45 minutes, stirring occasionally. If necessary, add boiling water during the cooking. Return chicken to rice and heat thoroughly.

THE LIBERIAN WAY OF COOKING

NOTE: *Rice should be loose and fluffy, not soggy. Cabbage wedges may be used instead of mixed vegetables. Add cabbage when flame has been reduced.*

JOLLOF RICE

1 CHICKEN (2 TO 2-1/2 LB.)
1 LB. STEWING BEEF
1 LB. SMOKED HAM OR BACON
2 ONIONS
LIBERIAN PEPPER (OPTIONAL)
3 OZ. TOMATO PASTE
1 C. COOKING OIL
1/2 TO 1 LB. VEGETABLES (FRESH OR FROZEN)
3 C. RICE
SALT AND BLACK PEPPER, TO TASTE

Cut up chicken, beef, and ham or bacon. Season with salt and black pepper. Flour and fry chicken and beef. Into Dutch oven or pot with heavy bottom, pour one cup oil (use oil in which chicken and beef have been fried). Sauté sliced onions and Liberian pepper (optional). To this, add meat, ham, and tomato paste, and stir well. If chicken is tough, it may be added at this time. Pour in a little more than the quantity of water required to cook the rice. Season with salt and black pepper. Cover, bring to a boil, and cook over low heat for 10 minutes. Add chicken (if tender), mixed vegetables, and rice. As soon as mixture starts to boil stir, add hot pepper if desired, reduce flame to lowest, and cook until rice is done. Raise from bottom and sides often to prevent sticking.

JOSEPH BARCHUE

Roland Svensson

Photo by: Mary Moran

Pigeon Peas and Rice

1 C. PIGEON PEAS
4 C. RICE
1 LB. SMOKED HAM, SALT PORK OR SALT
BEEF
2 T. FAT
1 MEDIUM ONION, DICED
BLACK PEPPER

Soak peas overnight in 3 cups of water. Drain peas. Boil salt beef or salt pork for 1 hour to remove excess salt. To one cup of meat stock, add four cups water. Cook peas in this until done. Add rice, onion, pepper, and boiled meat. Cook slowly on low flame. When almost done, pour in fat.

The Liberian Way of Cooking

74

BeTHaNY GIRLS' CHeCK RICe

2 C. UNCOOKED RICE
4 C. HOT WATER
1 TSP. SALT OR 1 BOUILLON CUBE

Put all ingredients into a pot and cook slowly for about 20 minutes. Stir after first 5 minutes of boiling. Then reduce heat and keep covered for the remaining cooking time.

The Check:
10 YOUNG HIBISCUS LEAVES
4 T. COLD WATER
PINCH OF BAKING SODA

Chop leaves finely and add to water and soda in small pot. Cover tightly and cook until all the water is gone. Put the cooked leaves into a bowl and chop with a spoon until you get a thick green mass. Working quickly, add the rice to the green mass mixing well. Add the rice until the color suits you. Serve this rice with any kind of gravy.

MILLY BAKER
PHEBE COOKBOOK

"Because of the crab, the crawfish will drink water.

MEANING:
If you want a project to be successful, get a big person to support it.

(When a crab gets up out of the wet sand there is a small waterspout.
The crawfish then gets his chance to run over and have a drink.)

KAREN'S BAKED PAWPAW WITH MEAT STUFFING

1 SMALL ONION, FINELY CHOPPED
1/2 TSP. FINELY CHOPPED GARLIC
21/2 T. VEGETABLE OIL
1 LB. GROUND BEEF
4 MEDIUM TOMATOES
1 TSP. FINELY CHOPPED HOT PEPPER
1 TSP. SALT
DASH OF BLACK PEPPER
5-6 LB. GREEN PAWPAW (PAPAYA)
CUT IN HALF LENGTHWISE AND SEEDED
3 T. GRATED CHEESE
2 C. BOILING WATER

Preheat oven to 350°F. Cook onions and garlic in oil in a frying pan until soft. Add beef and cook until all pink disappears. Add tomatoes, hot pepper, salt, and a little black pepper. Cook briskly, stirring occasionally, until most of the liquid is gone and mixture is thick. Taste for seasoning.

Spoon the mixture into the pawpaw shells. Place the shells side by side in a shallow baking pan. Put the pan in the middle of the oven and add enough boiling water to come about 1 inch up the sides of the pawpaw. Bake for one hour. Sprinkle each shell with cheese and bake for about 30 minutes more, until the pawpaw is easily pierced by a knife and the top is brown. To serve, transfer to heated dish and sprinkle with more cheese. This dish can be made with ripe pawpaw; in which case it need only cook in the oven for about 30 minutes.

REID HARVEY
COME LET'S EAT

Roland Svenson

Sitting quietly reveals crocodile's tricks.

STEWED PUMPKIN

2 LB. PUMPKIN
1/4 LB. MARGARINE OR VEGETABLE OIL
1 ONION (SLICED)
1/4 LB. COOKING BACON, CUT UP
2 C. WATER
BLACK PEPPER AND SALT TO TASTE

Peel pumpkin and dice. Sauté onions and bacon. Add pumpkin and brown lightly. Add water. Add salt, and pepper to taste. Let cook slowly on low fire for 30-40 minutes. Keep cooking until pumpkin is soft and mushy. Serve with meat or fish.

THE LIBERIAN WAY OF COOKING

LITTLE DEER MEETS MR. LEOPARD
A STORY BY ISAAC JOHNSON, MONROVIA

NEW DAY, MAY-JUNE 1967

Once upon a time, Little Deer and Leopard lived in the forest. Hungry time came often to Leopard and Little Deer. Food business was very hard.

One day Leopard had just finished eating a large, black deer. He was near Little Deer's eating place. Leopard decided to stay and rest there. Little Deer did not know Leopard was near his eating place. So Little Deer came and started eating his fresh leaves. When he lifted up his head, it was too late. Leopard was right before him and there was no way to run away.

Little Deer was so scared, but he tried hard to speak to Leopard. Leopard just looked at him and laughed. Little Deer wanted to run away. "Please let me go to my mother!" he begged. "Okay," said Leopard, "I will let you go if you can tell me three true things. If you fail, I shall eat you." "To begin with," said Little Deer, "if I knew you were here, I would not have come to eat today. Secondly, if you were hungry, you and I would not be talking like this. Thirdly, when I tell my family that I talked face to face with Mr. Leopard, they will not believe me."

When the clever Little Deer was finished talking, Leopard said: "All that you say is really true. Go home and be careful next time when you come to eat."

This story tells us why it is important to be sensible and clever while talking. Foolish talk can only get us in trouble.

SIDE DISHES

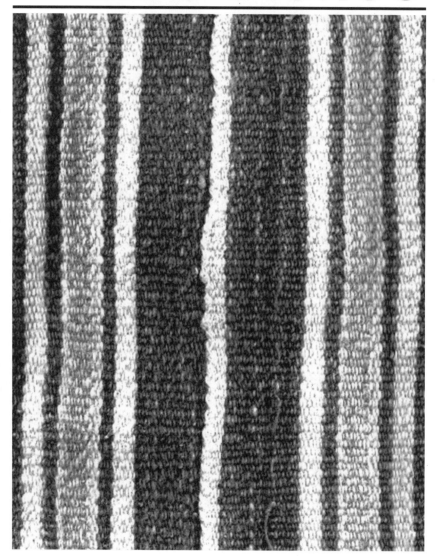

FUFU and DUMBOY

Fufu is a common dish throughout West Africa. It is usually made by boiling starchy foods such as cassava, plantain, or yams. The boiled food is then beaten in a large mortar and pestle until it forms a sticky mass. This is then served with one of the many soups. In Liberia, fufu is usually made from cassava that has fermented while dumboy is the fresh beaten cassava or other starchy root. For fufu, the cassava is peeled and grated very fine. The grated cassava is put into an empty flour sack and put under a press for about eight days until it has fermented. Fufu can also be bought in the market already fermented and formed into balls.

Some recipes are included for information only, as it is hardly expected that the readers will bring out the old mortar and pestle and start pounding. However, three substitute dumboy recipes are included, one of which can even be done in your microwave oven!

COOKED FUFU

10 BALLS OF FUFU
3 QT. COLD WATER

Dissolve fufu in cold water and strain, using a bamboo strainer or a sieve. Leave to settle for 30 minutes. Pour off liquid. Place sediment in saucepan and cook over low flame, stirring constantly with a wooden spoon until it thickens. Fufu is cooked when it changes from a white paste-like consistency to a more firm clear substance. Remove fufu from saucepan; put into a large bowl and allow to cool. Shape pieces of fufu into individual size balls. This is done by kneading each piece with your hand. Wet hands with cold water to keep fufu from sticking. Serve with a sauce, such as palaver, or soup. Serves about 6 persons.

THE LIBERIAN WAY OF COOKING

DUMBOY

Photo by: Joan Keenan

8-10 MEDIUM CASSAVA

Peel and wash cassava. Cover with water and boil until tender. Drain off water. Let cool. Cut up cassava into small pieces, about 1-1/2 to 2 inches long. Pound cassava in a wooden mortar with pestle, using very little water to moisten. Pound cassava until well crushed. Continue pounding until consistency is soft and smooth. During the final pounding for desired consistency, dip pestle into water at intervals. This makes the dumboy softer. Remove dumboy from mortar, shape into individual balls by kneading slightly, using a little cold water to make it smooth. Dumboy is eaten with soup. Serves about 6 persons.

THE LIBERIAN WAY OF COOKING

cassava

Cassava is an important staple food in Liberia, as well as in many other tropical countries. It is a long, slender root with a rough, dark brown skin. While rice is the food of choice for most Liberians, cassava is easy to grow and is especially welcome during the "hungry season" (about halfway through the rainy season) when rice is scarce. It can be planted with the rice or in a harvested rice field, and its root remains in the ground for up to two years before rotting. It can be treated like a potato, although it has a slightly stringy texture. It can be grated to make bread or roasted over an open fire, but it is most often used to make fufu and dumboy. The leaves are also used as cooking greens.

As with many of the foods from West Africa, cassava root can be purchased in any store specializing in Caribbean foods.

FUFU SUBSTITUTE

2-1/2 C. BISCUIT MIX
2-1/2 C. INSTANT POTATO FLAKES

Bring 6 cups of water to a rapid boil in a large, heavy pot. Combine the two ingredients and add to the water. Stir constantly for 10-15 minutes—a process that needs two people for best results: one to hold the pot while the other stirs vigorously with a strong implement (such as a thick wooden spoon). The mixture will become very thick and difficult to stir, but unless you are both vigilant and energetic, you'll get a lumpy mess. When fufu is ready (or you've stirred to the limits of your endurance!), dump about a cup of the mixture into a wet bowl and shake until it forms itself into a smooth ball. Serve on a large platter alongside a soup or stew.

THE AFRICA NEWS COOKBOOK

87

Photo by: Joan Keenan

NOTE: *Potato starch may be purchased in oriental food shops or stores that sell kosher foods.*

FUFU a La Keenan

2-1/2 C. INSTANT POTATO BUDS
2 C. POTATO STARCH
6 C. WATER

Combine ingredients in a large pot over low heat. Stir slowly for 15-20 minutes. Remove mixture from heat after it becomes a thick paste (dough-like). Place in moist bowl to cool. With wet hands (to prevent sticking), shape into a number of small balls. This can be served with peanut soup.

STEVE Keenan

Never drink soup that is so, so hot.

MEANING:
You must think about things before you act.

NOTE: *As with all microwave cooking, time will depend on your oven, so if fufu is not cooked, put back for a few more minutes. Use an extra half-cup water, if you like your fufu soft.*

MICROWAVE FUFU

1 C. INSTANT POTATO BUDS
1 C. POTATO STARCH
2 C. WATER

Mix ingredients until all the lumps disappear. Knead or, as we say in Liberia, work the fufu. Cover bowl and put in microwave for 5 minutes. Fufu is cooked when it changes from a white paste-like consistency to a more firm clear substance.

EMILY GUEGBEH PEAL AND **DR ROBERT MAYSON MD**

Photo by: Joan Keenan

BOILED CASSAVA

4 MEDIUM CASSAVA
4 C. WATER
1 TSP. SALT

Peel and wash cassava. Cut into 1-inch rounds. Put into water with salt and boil until tender. Drain off water and serve hot with butter or gravy.

ROASTED CASSAVA

4 MEDIUM CASSAVA
1 T. BUTTER
DASH SALT

Wash cassava well, leaving on skin. Put cassava on hot coals and let roast until tender. Cut cassava open lengthwise and butter while still hot. Sprinkle with a little salt.

Baked Cassava

4 MEDIUM CASSAVA
1 T. BUTTER
DASH OF SALT

Peel and wash cassava. Sprinkle with salt. Rub cassava with butter and bake in 375°F oven until cassava are cracked and brown. Using a pastry brush, butter cassava frequently while baking. Serve hot.

Fried Cassava

4 MEDIUM CASSAVA
4 C. WATER
SALT TO SEASON
2 C. COOKING OIL

Peel, wash, and cook cassava until tender. Let cool. Cut into strips (like French fried potatoes). Fry in deep, hot oil and drain on paper towels. Sprinkle with salt.

FRIED BANANAS

Slice peeled, half-ripe bananas into thin, lengthwise slices. Fry in deep oil until golden brown. Drain on paper towels.

FRIED RIPE PLANTAINS

3 RIPE PLANTAINS
2 C. COOKING OIL

Remove skins from plantains. Cut in half and then slice lengthwise into medium size slices. Fry slowly in deep fat until brown. Turn so both sides are browned. Be careful they do not burn. Drain on paper towels.

When bad luck calls your name, rotten banana will break your teeth.

Baked Ripe Plantains

4 RIPE PLANTAINS
2 T. BUTTER

Remove skins and brush on butter. Bake at 350°F, until plantains are tender and brown (about 30 - 40 min.). Can be served warm or cool.

Plantain Chips

Peel very green or half-ripe plantains and slice very thin. Fry in deep oil until golden and crisp. Drain on paper towels and sprinkle with salt. Keep in a sealed container.

94

Photo by:Vertez Burks

PLANTAIN DUMBOY

4 MEDIUM HALF-RIPE PLANTAINS
2 C. WATER
1/4 C. COOKING OIL

Wash plantains and boil in water until tender. Peel and cut up. Beat plantains in a wooden mortar with pestle, adding oil gradually. Pound plantains until soft and smooth. Serve with meat or fish dish and gravy.

THE LIBERIAN WAY OF COOKING

John Jones

Kelewele

2 TSP. GROUND GINGER
1/4 TSP. CAYENNE PEPPER
1/4 TSP. SALT (OPTIONAL)
2 T. WATER
4 RIPE PLANTAINS
1 C. VEGETABLE OIL, OR JUST ENOUGH FOR FRYING

In medium-size bowl, mix ginger, cayenne, salt, and water. Set aside. Peel plantains. Cut each plantain lengthwise into halves. Slice crosswise into 1-inch pieces. Add plantain to seasoning in bowl. Mix and let sit about 5 minutes. Drain well. In deep skillet, heat oil and add plantain in single layer. Fry until golden on all sides. About 5 minutes.

EMILY GUEGBEH PEAL
LIBERIAN COOKBOOK

96

*Crocodile can swim in the water a hundred years,
he will never be a fish.*

LIBERIAN SWEET POTATO PONE

3 C. GRATED RAW SWEET POTATOES
1 C. MOLASSES OR DARK CANE SYRUP
2 TSP. GRATED GINGER
2 TSP. BAKING SODA
1/2 TSP. SALT
1/3 C. OIL

Mix ingredients in a 3-quart sauce pan. Simmer slowly, stirring constantly for 10 minutes. Pour into a well-greased 9-inch baking pan and bake at 325°F for 30 minutes, stirring every 5 minutes for the first 20 minutes. Scrape sides of baking pan, smooth down the top, and continue to bake until nicely browned. Cut into squares and serve either hot or cold.

THE AFRICAN COOKBOOK

Eristus Mitchell

98

BOILED BREADFRUIT

1 FULL BREADFRUIT
3 C. WATER
1 TSP. SALT

Wash breadfruit and cut in wedges. Peel and cut into chunks. Boil in water with salt until done and tender. Breadfruit may also be cooked with the skin on for easier peeling.

FRIED BREADFRUIT

1 SMALL BREADFRUIT (HALF RIPE)
COOKING OIL FOR DEEP FRYING SALT TO SEASON

Peel and wash breadfruit. Slice into thin slices. Fry in deep fat until brown and tender. Drain on paper towels and sprinkle with salt if desired.

Anything that is eaten is not wasted.

MEANING:
Any kindness one does has some reward.

SWEET POTATO PUFFS

2 EGGS, BEATEN LIGHT
2 C. MASHED SWEET POTATOES
1 C. FLOUR
1-1/2 TSP. BAKING POWDER
1/2 TSP. SALT
1/4 TSP. GROUND CLOVES
1/4 TSP. CINNAMON
1/4 TSP. NUTMEG

Cook sweet potatoes until tender. Drain and mash. Let cool. Sift dry ingredients together. Beat eggs and potatoes together and add the dry ingredients. Roll out 1/2-inch thick, cut in circles, strips, or squares, and fry in deep fat like doughnuts, for 2-3 minutes. Drain and sprinkle with sugar while still warm.

TROPICAL COOKING

Betty Stull Schaffer

SWEET POTATO DREAMS

2 C. MASHED SWEET POTATOES
3 T. BUTTER
1 EGG, BEATEN
1/2 TSP. SALT
A FEW GRAINS OF BLACK PEPPER
BREAD CRUMBS

Cook sweet potatoes in a small amount of water until tender. Drain and mash. To mashed sweet potatoes, add the butter, egg, salt, and pepper. (If potatoes are very dry, add a small amount of hot milk to moisten.) Shape into small balls. Roll in bread crumbs. Fry in deep fat and drain. Serve with meat or fish.

THE LIBERIAN WAY OF COOKING

Town trap is not for rat alone...
it may be for the cows and goats and chickens as well.

MEANING:
This is powerful food for thought, that we are all interrelated
and what affects one could affect all.

There was an outcry about too many rats in this village. The humans set a trap in the only outlet of the rat community. The rats were starved as a result and began to call on other animals to disengage, or uncock, the trap. Cow said that it was not his business. Likewise goat, sheep, rooster, and all the rest. The rats remained without food.

Now a snake, trying to prey on the rats, was caught in the trap. The angry snake bit the chief's only daughter, who was passing by. She died. The trap was removed, and the snake killed. Then the chief ordered the chaining of cows, goats, sheep and roosters to be slaughtered to feed the many people attending the funeral. Rat circled around the animals, telling them, "If only you had listened and removed the trap for me, we could all be saved."

JOSEPH BARCHUE

EGGPLANT FRITTERS

1 LARGE EGGPLANT
1/2 TSP. SALT
1/2 TSP. PEPPER
3 EGGS, BEATEN
1/4 C. EVAPORATED WHOLE MILK
1 CUP FLOUR
OIL FOR FRYING

Boil unpeeled eggplant until soft. Cut in half and scoop out pulp. Mash well. Cool, then stir in salt, pepper, and eggs. Add milk and flour to make a stiff batter. (Use more milk or flour if necessary.) Drop by spoonfuls into hot deep oil. Turn when bottom browns. Remove when fully browned. Drain on paper towels. Serve hot.

THE LIBERIAN WAY OF COOKING

Cassava Croquettes

4 MEDIUM CASSAVA
4 C. WATER
1/4 C. CHOPPED ONIONS
1 EGG, BEATEN
2 T. MILK
1 T. BUTTER
2 T. FLOUR OR BREAD CRUMBS
SALT AND PEPPER TO TASTE
2 C. OIL FOR DEEP FRYING

Wash and peel cassava. Boil in two cups of water until tender and soft. Mash cassava and press through sieve to strain out strings. Add eggs, milk, salt, pepper, butter, and chopped onions to mashed cassava. Shape into small cakes using flour or bread crumbs to hold together. Fry in deep fat until brown and drain on paper towels. Serve hot.

The Liberian Way of Cooking

SPEAKING IN PARABLES
A STORY BY JOSEPH BARCHUE

Typical Liberian village teaching is rather indirect. A key element in the bush school is to learn to interpret and read between the lines. That draws the line between adult and non-adult conversation. One has to be keen in order to comprehend the adult language, because of the many parables and fables that are used.

For example, if a two- or three-year-old child begins to play with a candle flame, an adult usually remarks: "Well, son, I won't have to introduce an elephant to you. When you see it you will know it." As the child is growing up, he learns that elephant is the largest animal in the bush and its feet are as big as a large mortar. Amazingly, the child is usually the first to announce, "Here is an elephant!" when he sees one. He recognizes the size from the many descriptions he has heard.

Likewise, the candle; when the child's finger touches the flame of the candle, he then recognizes this is a fire. It is therefore a waste of time to keep him away in the first place, since he will do so from experience. Absolutely, this is not child abuse, but a form of conditioning.

DESSERTS

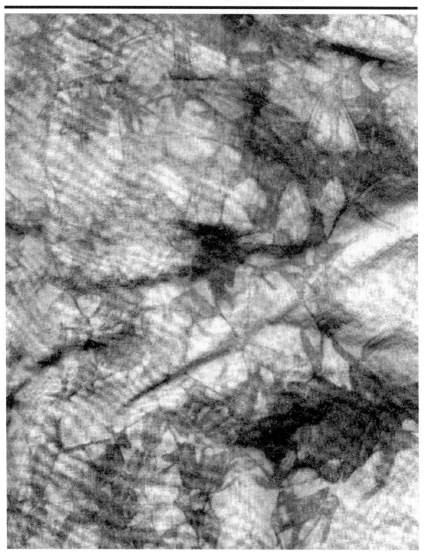

DESSERTS

109

Papaya Nut Cake

1/2 C. SHORTENING
1 C. SUGAR
1/4 C. DARK BROWN SUGAR
3 EGGS
1 C. HARD, YELLOW PAPAYA, SHREDDED
1/2 C. SOFT, RIPE PAPAYA, MASHED
1/3 TSP. PUMPKIN PIE SPICE
3-1/2 C. FLOUR, UNSIFTED ALL PURPOSE
4-1/2 TSP. BAKING POWDER
1 TSP. VANILLA EXTRACT
1/2 TSP. ALMOND EXTRACT
1-1/4 C. WALNUTS, CHOPPED
2 T. DARK MOLASSES
1 TSP. BAKING SODA
1 T. WATER
2 T. COOKING OIL
1 TSP. CINNAMON

Cream shortening and sugar until light. Add eggs, one at a time; beat well after each addition. Stir in papaya. Add 1 cup of walnuts. Combine flour, baking powder, and pumpkin pie spice. Sift and gradually add to egg/papaya mixture. Batter should be stiff. Combine water, molasses, baking soda, cooking oil, and cinnamon. Add almond and vanilla extract. Gently fold into cake batter. Pour into 9 x 9 x 1-3/4-inch pan. Sprinkle remaining chopped walnuts over top. Bake at 350°F for 50 minutes. Serves 12.

Native Recipes

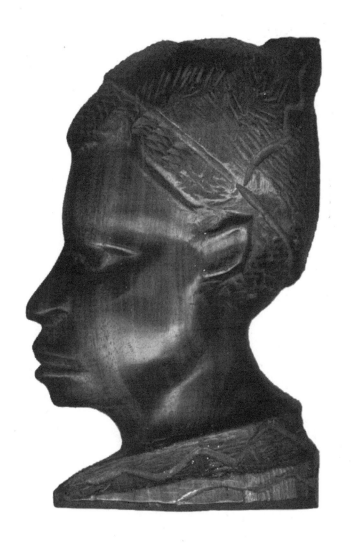

COCONUT ORANGE PUDDING

2 C. MILK
2 T. BUTTER
1 C. BREAD CRUMBS
2 EGG YOLKS
1/3 C. SUGAR
1/3 TSP. SALT
GRATED RIND OF 2 ORANGES
1-1/4 C. FRESH GRATED COCONUT
2 EGG WHITES
1/3 C. POWDERED SUGAR

Scald milk. Add bread crumbs and butter. Let mixture stand for 30 minutes. Beat egg yolks and mix in sugar, salt and half the grated orange rind. Add this mixture to the bread crumb mixture. Fold in 3/4 c. of coconut. Spoon mixture into greased custard cups and bake at 300°F for 40 minutes or until firm. Make a meringue, using the egg whites and powdered sugar. Add the remaining orange rind and spread on top of the pudding. Sprinkle with remaining coconut and bake 20 minutes or until coconut is slightly browned.

LIBERIAN COOKBOOK

PINEAPPLE PUDDING

1 MEDIUM PINEAPPLE
1 C. FLOUR
1/2 C. BUTTER
1 C. BROWN SUGAR
DASH OF SALT
TOPPINGS: CHOPPED WALNUTS,WHIPPED
CREAM, OR SOUR CREAM

Slice pineapple and cut up slices. Place them in a large pie pan or an 8-inch square cake pan. Mix the salt with about two tablespoons of brown sugar and sprinkle over pineapple. Make a topping by creaming the butter, flour, and remaining brown sugar. Spread it over the pineapple pieces. Bake for one hour at 300°F. Garnish with chopped walnuts and serve with whipped cream or sour cream, if desired.

THE LIBERIAN WAY OF COOKING

Betty Stull Schaffer

114

The testing of the pudding is the tasting of it.

MEANING:
Prove your capabilities instead of boasting about them.

COCONUT PUDDING

2 C. COCONUT MILK
1 C. COLD WATER
1/2 C. SUGAR
1/3 C. CORNSTARCH
2 T. NONFAT DRY MILK
PINCH OF SALT

Heat coconut milk to boiling. Mix all dry ingredients thoroughly. Add water and stir until smooth. Add this slowly to boiling coconut milk. Cook slowly, stirring constantly until thick. Pour into an 8-inch square pan and let cool. Cut into 2-inch squares.

THE LIBERIAN WAY OF COOKING

Roland Svensson

PAPAYA PUDDING

4 PAPAYAS (SMALL)
1 C. CRUSHED PINEAPPLE
3 T. CORNSTARCH
3/4 C. SUGAR
1 TSP. VANILLA

Cut papayas in half. Remove seeds. Scoop out papaya, mash slightly and put into saucepan. Drain pineapple and add it to the papaya. Cook slowly for 30 minutes, stirring occasionally. Add a little cold water to the cornstarch to make a paste, add to the papaya mixture and stir until thick and clear. Stir in sugar and vanilla. Spoon into dessert dishes and chill.

THE LIBERIAN WAY OF COOKING

A rat that wants a full stomach should not be afraid of getting wet.

STEWED MANGOES WITH CLOVES

4 LARGE MANGOES
1 C. SYRUP FROM CANNED PEACHES
6 WHOLE CLOVES

Peel mangoes and cut in large pieces. Put mangoes, syrup, and cloves in a one-quart saucepan and simmer for 15 minutes, or until mangoes are tender. Spear some of the pieces with a few cloves, cool and serve in compote dishes.

THE AFRICAN COOKBOOK

COCONUT PIE

1-1/2 C. GRATED FRESH COCONUT
1/2 C. SUGAR
3/4 C. BUTTER
2 EGGS
1 TSP. VANILLA
1/4 TSP. BAKING SODA
1 C. MILK
1/4 TSP. NUTMEG
1 PIE SHELL, UNBAKED

Cream butter and sugar well. Beat eggs until frothy and blend well with sugar and butter mixture. Add baking soda, vanilla, nutmeg, and milk. Bake pie shell five minutes or until partially brown. Pour ingredients into partially baked pie shell. Cover top with strips of crust. Flute edges. Bake at 350°F for about 40 minutes, or until golden brown.

THE LIBERIAN WAY OF COOKING

Betty Stull Schaffer

On FInDInG FOOD In a VILLaGe

The day we moved to Klay, I walked through the village looking for the market. I had in mind a modest version of the big fresh produce market in Monrovia. There was not market to be found. In fact, there was no food. I saw a few bananas, one pawpaw, and a small pile of about five peppers. It was pretty discouraging. I inquired on all sides about oranges, grapefruit, pineapple, butter pear, and so on. People were most friendly and pleasant, but no one seemed to have any definite notion of how I might get some. I came home with the idea that there was nothing to be had in this area. We lived on canned food, supplemented by an occasional banana, that pawpaw, and those five peppers for the first week or so. Then people began to come to my door. A man with a big basket of grapefruit appeared. I was so delighted, I bought all the fruit and the basket as well. I also learned that there were a number of grapefruit and orange trees near an old mission, no longer in use. Little by little I began to get oranges, limes, pineapple, cucumbers, country tomatoes, eddo, coconuts, all sorts of things that had been nowhere in sight. Soon the word spread that we were a sure-fire market for local produce. Along with the fruits and vegetables, we began to get people selling mats, baskets, carvings, and one man came proudly bringing a small boa constrictor I could have had cheap.

KaTHY D'azeveDO
KWI STYLE COOKING

ORANGE TARTS

1 RIPE ORANGE
3 T. WHITE SUGAR
1 T. BROWN SUGAR
2 T. BUTTER
2 T. CAKE OR BISCUIT CRUMBS
1 EGG
1/2 C. ORANGE MARMALADE
8 OZ. PIE CRUST

Line tart pans with pastry and prick well. Bake in 350°F oven for about 5 minutes. Grate the peel of the orange. Cut the orange and squeeze out the juice. Put sugar in a small saucepan with butter, orange juice, and rind. Stir in the crumbs and well-beaten egg. Cook over gentle heat, stirring constantly until mixture is thick. Let cool. Spread a thin layer of marmalade on the pastry shells and add the orange mixture. Bake at 350°F for 15 minutes.

THE LIBERIAN WAY OF COOKING

Roland Svensson

LIBERIAN QUILTERS

Liberia's first American settlers were women who brought with them the practical and beautiful craft of quilting. Some had undoubtedly learned this in their unpaid work before gaining their freedom and embarking on the perilous journey to Africa. Like many female immigrants of the 19th and early 20th century, they would describe themselves by skill in entry documents as "seamstress." Some of the earliest settler ships' manifests in Monrovia included seamstresses. Today, the quilters of Liberia hail from the coastal communities where many of the first American immigrants settled: Greenville, Paynesville, Arthington and in pockets around Grand Bassa and Sinoe counties. Their designs include variations on traditional American and British patterns, some of them obviously passed down by memory, others culled from magazines and quilting books. Like quilters everywhere, Liberian women preserve their world in vibrant depictions of the flora and fauna of West Africa as well. As Liberian quilts became collectors items for travelers and visiting workers, co-ops were formed to maximize the financial benefits for communities. Unfortunately, many of the "settler communities" were hit hard in the civil war and many of the quilters fled to Monrovia, where once again they formed cooperatives and continue the legacy that by now has become a livelihood. Friends of Liberia is in touch with some of the new workshops and can make the connection for U.S. quilt enthusiasts eager to be part of this creative and resilient tradition.

PAT REILLY

124

Photo by: Joan Keenan

maNGO PIE

6-8 RIPE MANGOES
1/2 C. SUGAR
1 TSP. CINNAMON
1/4 TSP. SALT
1/4 TSP. NUTMEG
1 T. FLOUR
1 T. BUTTER
TOP AND BOTTOM PIE CRUST

Wash, peel, and slice mangoes. Fill unbaked pie shell with the mangoes. Sprinkle the sugar, cinnamon, flour, nutmeg, and salt over the fruit and dot with butter. Put on the top crust or a lattice crust. Bake at 425°F for about 45 minutes or until the crust is golden brown.

THE LIBERIAN WAY OF COOKING

COCONUT TARTS

1 C. GRATED FRESH COCONUT
1/2 C. BUTTER
1/2 C. SUGAR
2 EGGS
1 TSP. VANILLA
1/2 C. CREAM
OR EVAPORATED WHOLE MILK
DASH OF BAKING SODA
1/4 TSP. NUTMEG
18 PRE-BAKED TART SHELLS

Cream butter and sugar. Separate egg yolks and whites. Beat egg yolks and add to butter and sugar. Beat in coconut. Add the cream, vanilla, and nutmeg. Beat egg whites and baking soda until stiff. Fold into yolk mixture. Pour mixture into pre-baked tart shells and bake at 375°F until brown. Makes about 18 tarts.

THE LIBERIAN WAY OF COOKING

FRUIT PIE

2 C. MILK
1 C. SUGAR
1/2 C. FLOUR
1/4 TSP. SALT
3 EGG YOLKS
2 T. BUTTER
2 T. LEMON JUICE
1-1/2 C. GRATED COCONUT
1 C. CRUSHED PINEAPPLE (DRAINED)
1 PIE SHELL, BAKED

Sift together sugar, salt, and flour in a bowl. Separate yolk and white of eggs. Beat the egg yolks and add to the dry ingredients. Scald milk in top part of double boiler, and gradually pour hot milk over mixture, stirring constantly. Return to double boiler and cook for 4 minutes. Add butter, lemon juice, pineapple, and coconut. Cool. Pour into a baked pie shell and top with meringue.

Meringue:
6 T. SUGAR
3 EGG WHITES

Beat egg whites until stiff. Gradually add sugar, beating constantly. Spoon out on top of pie. Bake for 10-12 minutes at 350°F.

THE LIBERIAN WAY OF COOKING

Banana Tart

1 C. MILK
2 T. FLOUR
2 EGGS
2 RIPE BANANAS
1/2 C. SUGAR
1/8 TSP. SALT
1 TSP. LEMON JUICE
1/2 TSP. LEMON EXTRACT
1 PIE SHELL, BAKED

Sift together the flour, salt, and 1/4 cup of sugar. Separate yolk and white of eggs. Beat the egg yolks and add to the dry ingredients. Heat the milk and add to mixture gradually. Pour mixture into top part of a double boiler and cook over hot water, stirring constantly for about 15 minutes or until mixture thickens. Slice bananas and add. Stir in the lemon juice. Set aside to cool.

Beat egg whites until stiff. Fold in remaining sugar and lemon extract. Put banana mixture into pastry crust and cover with egg white mixture. Bake for 10-12 minutes at 325°F. Serve cold.

THE LIBERIAN WAY OF COOKING

Photo by: Edith Gordon

PINEAPPLE PIE

2-1/2 C. FRESH PINEAPPLE
(CRUSHED)
2 EGGS
1 C. SUGAR
1 T. LIME JUICE
1 T. BUTTER
1 9-IN. PIE SHELL,
UNBAKED

Beat eggs, add sugar and lime juice. Combine the egg mixture and the crushed pineapple. Pour the filling into an unbaked pie shell and dot with butter. Moisten the edge of the pastry with water, cover with top crust. Trim and press edges together with the tines of a fork. Prick top crust with fork to allow steam to escape. Bake 10 minutes at 425°F. Reduce heat to 350°F and bake until brown. Makes one 9-inch pie.

THE LIBERIAN WAY OF COOKING

129

PaWPaW (PAPAYA) PIE

2 MEDIUM PAWPAW (PAPAYAS)
1/2 C. SUGAR
2 TSP. LIME JUICE
1/4 TSP. CINNAMON
1 TSP. VANILLA
DASH OF SALT
1/2 TSP. NUTMEG
2 T. BUTTER (MELTED)
1 PIE SHELL, UNBAKED

Wash, peel, and dice pawpaw. Boil in enough water to cover, until well done. Drain off the water and run the pawpaw through a sieve or mash it well. Add the sugar, lime juice, cinnamon, vanilla, salt, nutmeg, and melted butter. Mix thoroughly and pour mixture into an unbaked pie crust. Bake at 400°F for about 45 minutes, until the crust is golden brown. Makes 8 servings.

THE LIBERIAN WAY OF COOKING

SWEET POTATO PIE

3 C. MASHED SWEET POTATOES
1/2 C. SUGAR
3/4 C. BUTTER
1-1/4 C. MILK
2 EGGS
1 TSP. VANILLA
1/2 TSP. GRATED NUTMEG
1 9-IN. PIE SHELL, UNBAKED

Wash sweet potatoes, peel, and cut into cubes. Cook until tender. Drain off excess water and mash. Cream butter and sugar thoroughly, until fluffy. Add beaten eggs, milk, mashed potatoes, and nutmeg. Stir vigorously until mixture is smooth. Pour into an unbaked pie shell. Bake at 425°F about 10 minutes, until crust begins to brown. Reduce the heat and bake at 375°F about 45 minutes, until pie filling is firm and crust is a golden brown. Makes one 9-inch pie.

THE LIBERIAN WAY OF COOKING

Roland Svensson

PUMPKIN PIE

1-1/2 C. FRESH COOKED PUMPKIN
3/4 C. SUGAR
1/2 TSP. GINGER
1 TSP. CINNAMON
1-1/4 C. MILK
3/4 TSP. SALT
1/4 TSP. NUTMEG
3 EGGS, BEATEN
3/4 C. EVAPORATED WHOLE MILK
OR HEAVY CREAM
1 9-IN. PIE SHELL, UNBAKED

Peel the pumpkin and cut in cubes. Cook in small amount of water until tender. Drain off water and mash or press through a sieve. Add all other ingredients. Mix well and pour into an unbaked pie shell. Bake for 10 minutes at 450°F, reduce heat to 350°F and bake until a knife inserted comes out clean, about 35 minutes. Makes one 9-inch pie.

THE LIBERIAN WAY OF COOKING

PAPAYA COCONUT PIE

1-1/2 C. SUGAR
1/2 TSP. SALT
1/2 TSP. CINNAMON
1/4 TSP. CLOVES
2 EGGS, BEATEN
1 C. EVAPORATED MILK
1-1/2 C. STEWED PAPAYA,
PUT THROUGH SIEVE
1/4 C. COCONUT, COARSELY GRATED
1/2 C. COCONUT, FINELY GRATED
2 TSP. HONEY
1 PIE SHELL, UNBAKED

Mix first 8 ingredients in order given. Fill unbaked pie shell and bake at 450°F for about 15 minutes, then at 350°F for about 30 minutes, until knife inserted comes out clean. When nearly cooked, top with remaining coconut. Drizzle on warmed honey and return to oven to brown delicately. Serves 8.

NATIVE RECIPES

Are you trading your set of teeth for palm kernels?
What will you chew the kernels with after you get them?

MEANING:
This implies a great sacrifice for a goal
that may not be worth the sacrifice itself.

SOURSOP SHERBET

1 MEDIUM SOURSOP
4 OZ. EVAPORATED WHOLE MILK
1 C. SUGAR
DASH NUTMEG
1 C. WARM WATER

Cut and peel soursop. Place pieces in pan with warm water. Pass the soursop through a sieve. Add sugar, milk and nutmeg. Blend well. Freeze. Makes 6 servings.

JOAN KEENAN

Papaya Ice

2 C. MASHED PAPAYA PULP
1/2 C. WATER
JUICE OF ONE LEMON
JUICE OF ONE GRAPEFRUIT
3/4 C. SUGAR

Mix ingredients together. Place mixture in shallow pan in freezer, until it is firm at the edges. Beat with electric mixer until well mixed. Return to freezer until firm. Makes 4 servings.

VARIATION: *Use orange juice instead of grapefruit juice, or squeeze in the juice of a very ripe mango.*

Joan Keenan

A dog will not forsake its owner to follow a king.

MANGO SHIMMY

1 PKG. ORANGE GELATIN
1-1/2 C. ORANGE JUICE
1/2 C. WATER
1 C. MANGO, DICED
1 T. SUGAR
1 LEMON

Place diced mango in sauce pan and sprinkle with sugar and lemon juice. Simmer gently for 5 minutes and set aside.
Place orange juice and water in sauce pan, heat to boiling, add gelatin and stir until dissolved. Chill until slightly thick. Fold in mango. Pour into individual molds and chill until firm. Garnish with whipped cream and cherries.

THE LIBERIAN WAY OF COOKING

NOTE: *You may need to place peels in front of a fan or in an air-conditioned room to dry if the weather is too humid.*

CANDIED GRAPEFRUIT RIND

1 GRAPEFRUIT RIND
1-1/2 C. WATER
1 C. SUGAR

Cut grapefruit rind into thin strips. Add water to cover. Boil 10 minutes. Pour off water. Add more water and boil for 10 more minutes. Drain. Add ½ cup water and 1 cup of sugar to well-drained peels. Cook slowly, stirring constantly until syrup is absorbed. Spread on waxed paper to dry. Then roll in sugar.

VIRGINIA BOWERS
PHEBE COOKBOOK

Photo by: Phillip Robinson

Ivan Butcher

PAPAYA CANDY

2 MEDIUM GREEN PAPAYAS,
GRATED
2 C. SUGAR
1 T. LIME JUICE
1 TSP. ORANGE PEEL
1/2 C. WATER

Combine papaya with enough water to cover. Boil for 2 minutes. Strain and repeat procedure two more times. Then drain well. Combine sugar and 1/2 cup water. Boil until the syrup forms a thread in a glass of cold water. Add the papaya and simmer until the mixture leaves the side of the pan. Stir in the lime juice and orange peel. Pour the mixture onto a buttered platter. Cool and shape into balls. Then roll the balls in sugar.

NATIVE RECIPES

COCONUT CANDY

2 FRESH COCONUTS,
  PEELED AND SLICED VERY THIN (POTATO PEELER WORKS WELL)
1 C. BROWN SUGAR
1 C. WHITE SUGAR
2/3 C. WATER
2 T. CORN SYRUP
1 INCH FRESH GINGER ROOT,
  PEELED AND FINELY GRATED

Toast coconut in oven until crisp and lightly browned. Combine remaining ingredients for syrup and cook without stirring until syrup reaches 290°F (or until drops in cold water become brittle). Remove from heat and quickly add coconut, stirring as little as possible. Pour out onto greased cookie sheets and spread thinly. As candy begins to cool and harden, cut into small pieces.

DORIS BOMBERGER
PHEBE COOKBOOK

141

Sesame Seasoning

3 C. SESAME SEEDS
SALT (OPTIONAL)

Put dried seeds in a heavy skillet and place over a low flame. Stir continuously, until brown. Sprinkle very lightly with salt, then pound until most of the seeds, but not all, are crushed. Store in a jar until ready to use. Can be used in pie crusts or soup for rice, just about anything you can think of.

HWI STYLE COOKING

Bananas and Sesame Seeds

BANANAS
LIME JUICE
SESAME SEASONING
BROWN SUGAR

Cut bananas into 1-inch pieces. Dip in lime juice, then in equal parts of crushed sesame seasoning and brown sugar.

HWI STYLE COOKING

Benne seed candy

Betty Stull Schaffer

1 C. SUGAR
1/3 C. WATER
1-1/2 TEASPOONS BUTTER
1 C. BENNE (SESAME) SEEDS, TOASTED

Butter baking sheet. Cook sugar and water in heavy medium saucepan over low heat, stirring until sugar dissolves. Increase heat and boil without stirring until syrup turns dark amber color, swirling pan occasionally and washing down sugar crystals on side of pan with wet pastry brush, about 13 minutes. Mix in butter, then sesame seeds. Immediately pour mixture onto prepared sheet. Cool completely. Break into pieces.

NOTE: *Benne, or sesame seeds, are popular in southern cooking today. They were most likely brought to the U.S. by enslaved Africans in the 1600's.*

Vana Prewitt

143

He who cannot dance finds fault with the beating of the drums.

sesame cookies

1/2 C. SHORTENING
3 T. SUGAR
1 TSP. VANILLA
1 C. SESAME SEASONING (SEE RECIPE P.142)
1 C. FLOUR

Cream shortening and sugar. Blend in vanilla and then sesame seasoning. Add flour and mix well. Form the dough into small balls the size of a walnut. Bake them in a slow oven for about 45 minutes. Roll in powdered sugar, cool and store in air tight container.

KWI STYLE COOKING

KALLAH

Photo by: Phillip Robinson

(ALSO CALLED A LIBERIAN DONUT)

1/2 5-LB. BAG SELF-RISING FLOUR
1 EGG
1-1/2 CUPS SUGAR
NUTMEG AND/OR CINNAMON, IF DESIRED
WATER TO MAKE A MANAGEABLE DOUGH
(NOT TOO STICKY OR RUNNY)

Use hands or ice cream scoop to shape dough into balls and drop into hot oil. Deep fry until deeply golden. Lift out with slotted spoon and cool on paper towels to absorb excess oil. May roll in more sugar, if desired. Makes a couple of dozen good-size Kallah.

NOTE: *Kallah is one of Karen's favorite Liberian snack food. She used to get it at a roadside stand*

KAREN DAHN

GLOSSARY

Benne seed (benni seed) - Sesame seeds.

Bonnies - Dried bony herring.

Breadfruit - Large round or oval tropical fruit with a starch whitish pulp. See picture p. 98.

Butter pear - Avocado.

Cassava (sweet) - A tropical plant with edible starchy roots. See p. 86.

Cassava leaf - Leaves of the cassava plant. Cooked as a green vegetable.

Coconut milk - Milk-like substance extracted when hot water is poured over fresh, grated coconuts.

Coconut water - Clear liquid inside of the green or ripe coconuts.

Crawfish - Crayfish, freshwater crustacean. Regular shrimp may be substituted.

Dumboy - Heavy starchy substance made from boiled, pounded sweet cassavas or other root crop. See p.83.

Eddoe - Underground tuberous root. Eaten like potato. In the Caribbean, one of the ground provisions, or edible root crops.

Fufu - Starchy food made from fermented cassava. See p. 83.

Groundnut (Peanut) - Pounded into a paste and used in cooking, as well as roasted.

Liberian Rice - country rice, similar to brown rice. Delicious when cooked properly.

Mango - A yellow-red tropical fruit with a thick rind and a sweet, juicy, yellow pulp.

Palm butter - A stew made from the nuts of the oil palm tree.

Palm cabbage - Palm hearts.

Palm nuts - Nuts from the oil palm tree.

146

Palm oil - Reddish oil extracted from palm nuts. This oil has a distinctive flavor. Can be purchased in African-Caribbean specialty food stores.

Palm wine - A fermented drink, extracted from the oil palm tree. See p.22.

Papaya - A melon-like tropical fruit that rages from light yellowish through deep yellow, to orange, when ripe. May also be cooked green as a vegetable. The latex of the green fruit contains papain, a protein-digesting enzyme that acts as a meat tenderizer. Available in some super markets or Caribbean specialty stores.

Pawpaw - See papaya.

Plantain - A tropical plant that has a fruit resembling the banana. It must be cooked before eating.

Platto leaves - The leaves of a green vegetable having a slimy substance.

Potato greens - The leaves of the sweet potato plant. Cooked as a green vegetable.

Soursop - A large tropical fruit shaped like a kidney and covered with soft green prickles. The white pulp is sweet and juicy, but contains many large black seeds.

Stock fish - A codfish cured by being hung in the open air to dry.

Sweet potato - A tropical trailing plant with a large fleshy orange or yellow root, used as a vegetable. The leaves are also used for cooking as a green vegetable.

Tripe - Part of the stomach of an ox, steer or cow, used as food.

Yam - The edible, starchy, tuberous root of a tropical climbing plant. One of the Caribbean ground provisions. Not to be confused with what Americans call yams, which are sweet potatoes.

WHO'S WHO
IN LIBERIAN COOKHOUSE COOKING

IN LIBERIAN COOKHOUSE COOKING

Kathy d'Azevedo of Reno, Nev., is the author of "Kwi Style Cooking," which came out of her and her husband Warren's first anthropological field work in Liberia in the late 1950s. They were both involved in training the first group of Peace Corps volunteers for Liberia in 1962. "The girls asked how do we cook? What do we do?" she recalls about why she wrote the cookbook. "To my amazement it was copied and it took off. It went to everybody. Nobody ever asked if it was OK, but it was OK." She subsequently became very interested in Liberian food and it became the basis for a field trip in the 1980s. The d'Azevedos have both written extensively on Liberia and Liberians but it is the much-copied cookbook that endeared Kathy to generations of Peace Corps volunteers and others grappling with new foods in the new setting.

Joseph P. Barchue of Kokoyah, Bong County, Liberia, began his travels with a couple of Peace Corps volunteers to Gbarnga and on to Buchanan. As a result of financial assistance from his Peace Corps friends, he obtained his middle and high school education in private schools in Liberia and later trained as a physician's assistant. He took up his first assignment with the Leprosy Control Program and then was hired by a River Blindness research group from the United States. "As we began to expand in other areas of biomedical research, such as HIV and related interests, the civil war commenced, putting an end to our progress," he recalls. Joseph migrated to the United States with an American colleague. He furthered his education in Health Administration but maintained his career in research.

148

He is currently a Research Associate in the Department of Medicine/ Cardiology, University of Alabama at Birmingham.

Albert Bropleh lived for several years in Overland Park, Kan., and worked for Network Technical Engineer Enhanced Platform Services with Sprint. He returned to Liberia in 2007 to serve as Chairman of the Liberian Telecommunications Authority. He sent copies of parables from a book he used as a student in Liberia.

Vertez Burks lives in San Diego, where she is a technician and media specialist. She was a Peace Corps volunteer teacher in Owensgrove, Liberia, 1965-1967. She then taught on St. Croix from 1969 until 1995. She remembers taking the picture of her roommate on the monkey bridge: "I took the picture because no one else was there and she needed someone to tell the story if the bridge gave way!"

Ivan Butcher notes that his father is African-Caribbean from Trinidad and his grandfather is from Barbados and his grandmother from Grenada. Ivan's mother is from Appomattox, Va., her father was African-American and her mother descended from Cherokee Indians. Ivan grew up in the inner-city of New York and went to St. Croix to teach art after finishing school in 1969. He has retired and is still actively involved in the island community.

Karen Warren Dahn was a Peace Corps teacher at B.W. Harris Episcopal School in Monrovia and later at W.V.S. Tubman High School. She worked for two more years on private contract, teaching English and African literature at St.

Patrick's High School. She married Marcus Dahn, had a son, Michael, and returned to Liberia with a master's in TESOL from Columbia Teachers College in 1983. She served as Assistant Peace Corps Director/Education and had a daughter, Miaghen. They transferred with Peace Corps to Lesotho. Since 1988, the family has lived in Athens, Ohio, where Karen is Assistant to the Dean of the College of Arts and Sciences and has completed two more master's degrees and her doctorate.

Carl Dealy of Fresno, Calif., was a Peace Corps volunteer "fish head," 1984-1987, promoting inland fisheries for the Nimba County Rural Development Project, first in Duo, Zahn Clan, Nimba County, and later throughout the country. His wife, Kou, is from Nimba. The father of two boys, he notes that one of the great tragedies of the civil war was that child soldiers "probably have no concept of the rich history and gentle customs of their own country."

Esther Warner Dendel (1910-2002) was author of twelve books, many of them emanating from her life in Liberia with her husband from 1941 to 1944. She went on many walking trips in the hinterland. Whether at home or exploring, she would trade stories with her Liberian companions: one European or American story for one Liberian story. Her last book, "You Can't Unsneeze a Sneeze," is a compilation of many of the Liberian stories she collected and the circumstances of the trades. She also expressed her artistry with fabrics, fabric design, textiles and pottery in her California studio.

Laurie Funk's husband, Dave, was in Nimba County, Liberia, with the Peace Corps from 1987 to 1989. Laurie spent nine weeks there with him one summer and four weeks the next.

Edith Gordon was a Peace Corps volunteer teacher at Kingville (No. 7), Liberia, 1965-1967. After Peace Corps service, she moved to St. Croix, where she has taught and served as a librarian from 1969 to 2003. Now a grandmother, she is retired and plans to spend time traveling again.

Dorothy Wrase Hares, R.D., of Baldwinsville, N.Y., worked as a Peace Corps volunteer at JFK hospital in Liberia 1971-1973 and as a dietician at a major hospital in Syracuse, N.Y. A native of Minnesota, Dorothy has degrees from University of Iowa and Syracuse University. She is married to Bill Hares, who was a Peace Corps teacher at Bassa High School in Buchanan, 1973-1974. They have a son, Ben. Dorothy, besides being a dietician, is an enthusiastic cook.

Charles Hartwig was a Peace Corps volunteer in Liberia, 1965-67, working with a public administration project in Monrovia, most of the time in the Treasury Department . He also taught a history class at the night high school at the University of Liberia. He recalls, " I didn't get out of Monrovia too much, but then when my wife and I taught at Cuttington in 1985 and 1986, we seldom got down to Monrovia. We witnessed the election in October 1985, perhaps the last chance that Liberia had to avoid the disasters that began a few years later." Their daughter was a Peace Corps volunteer in Lesotho.

Reid Harvey lived in both Robertsport and Monrovia, Liberia, from 1971 to 1982, working on an art glass project and several ceramic processes. A graduate of the New York State

College of Ceramics at Alfred University, his primary interest is in appropriate technology. He has worked in Liberia, Sudan, Kenya, Guinea, the Ivory Coast, Bangladesh and Nepal, and other third world countries.

Carol and Don Hegman were Peace Corps volunteers in Liberia from 1968 to 1972. They lived first in New Krutown, just north of Monrovia, and taught elementary school. They then moved north to Tappita, where Carol worked on teacher education and Don worked on a social studies project for the Department of Education.

Steve Hirst and his wife, Lois, were Peace Corps volunteers in Tappita with the first group to serve in Liberia. In the mid-1970s, they worked in Havasu Canyon in the American west. He is the author of the famous pepper plant story included in this book and has shared Liberian pepper seeds as a celebration of the last peace accord with others as far away as the Ukraine. The Hirsts both worked at Northern Michigan University in Marquette, where Lois chaired the educational administration program and Steve was with the Seaborg Center for Science and mathematics. They now live in Flagstaff, Ariz., where they lead hikes as U.S. Forest Service interpretive rangers.

Sally Gosline Humphrey served in the Peace Corps in Tumutu from 1963-1965. She is the author of a children's book, "A Family in Liberia". She now lives in Oxford, England.

John Obafemi Jones is a professional artist and art educator who has been teaching in the Virgin Islands since 1979. A graduate of Fisk University, he has had art shows both in the

Virgin Islands and stateside. He shows his work in the Densau art gallery in Atlanta and Simply Art in New York. John has long been interested in West African issues, so he was very willing to support the cookbook by contributing his art. Now he's just waiting to try a recipe!

Joan Keenan was a Peace Corps volunteer teacher in Owensgrove, Grand Bassa County, Liberia, 1965-1967. Shortly after Peace Corps service, she began teaching on St. Croix with three other former volunteers. She intended to stay on St. Croix for a short time, but that was in 1969! Her favorite dish is collard greens and chicken. She got started compiling this cookbook after getting information on Friends of Liberia through the Internet in 1995. She is now retired after 36 years of teaching and producing a documentary film on World War II veterans of the Virgin Islands.

Steve Keenan of Jordan, N.Y., joined the Peace Corps after graduating from college in 1963. He taught school in Liberia. He has worked for CARE in Egypt, and traveled extensively in Africa, Europe, and North America. He and his wife, Jackie, married in Liberia and reside in Central New York. He recently published a book, "Soujourns in West Africa".

John and Lyn Kucij, of Schenectady, N.Y., were Peace Corps volunteers in Voinjama, 1970-73. They returned to Liberia for a visit in 1987, bringing their two sons to meet their old friends. The Kucijes remember Liberia as a safe peaceful place. They have raised thousands of dollars for Friends of Liberia by hosting the annual African Dinner at Hudson Valley Community College. John is a former board member of FOL.

Dr. Robert P. Mayson is from Lexington, Sinoe County. He is an obstetrician in Freehold, N.J. His sister, Emily Guegbeh Peal, says that he loves to cook on weekends and holidays.

Eristus Mitchell is a graduate of St. Croix Central High School. He won several prizes in local student art contests and generously agreed to sketch the banana plant and breadfruit tree for the cookbook.

Mary Moran is an Professor of Anthropology and Africana and Latin American Studies at Colgate University who lived in Gbenelu, Cape Palmas, Liberia, for 16 months in 1982 and 1983, doing research for her dissertation at Brown University. Her subject was the cultural construction of gender and other forms of prestige hierarchies among the Grebo.

Sheree Morgan of Northhampton, Mass., taught chemistry and math at W.D. Coleman High School in Clay-Ashland, Montserrado County, 1989-1990. She has spent some time in graduate school, taught chemistry labs and did publicity work for a women's studies research center before starting dental school in 1997. She is currently a dentist practicing in Latham, N.Y.

Agnes Peabody of Centerville, Va., was born in Monrovia. Her mother was mayor of Marshall City, the first woman to hold a mayoral position in Liberia. Her father was an attorney and rubber farmer and also served in government. Angela was a broadcast journalist before moving to the United States in 1980, where she also worked for WHUR Radio and WPGC-AM Business Radio in the Washington D.C. area. She has also

154

worked as a travel consultant in Arlington, Va. She has two sons and has this to say about parenting: "Although my sons grew up in the States, the family and I have always tried to teach them the Liberian traditions that have helped us survive the obstacles today."

Emily Guebeh Peal of Temecula, Calif., has a master's in administration from Michigan State and works in the administration of the University of California at San Diego. "While at Michigan, I invited a lot of American friends over for dinner, they said the food was so good that they encouraged me to write a cook book," she told FOL on generously lending her recipes to this effort. She is a tireless worker for the Society for the Conservation of Nature in Liberia. Her husband, Alex, is director of their Liberian operations.

Vana Prewitt is a training coordinator for North Carolina. In Liberia, in the mid-1980s, she worked at the Liberian Rural Communications Network as an educational radio producer and trainer. She remembers: "My apartment was on 9th street in Sinkor, next to the beach, about a block from the USAID office and a mile from the President's house. To save my sanity, I took the moneybus upcountry to Robertsport to visit friends once a month...My cat, Chester, woke me up the morning of the coup attempt in 1985, November. He was sitting in the window and just screaming at the top of his lungs about 4:30 a.m. when the fighting started along Tubman Boulevard."

Pat Reilly, of Marshall, Va., was a Peace Corps teacher in Buchanan, Liberia, 1973-74, and later a Peace Corps recruiter in New York City and at Ohio University. She served as

Chairman of the Board of the National Peace Corps Association from 2003-2004. She has been on the Executive Committee of Friends of Liberia since 1990. She spent 20 years as a newspaper editor and reporter and helped to edit this cookbook. She now works for the U.S. government as a communicator and is married to Richard Irish, a former Peace Corps volunteer in the Philippines. She says of editing this book, "FOL has introduced me to hundreds of ex-PCVs from Peace Corps' 30-year life in Liberia and, as different as they all are, I can safely say they have a couple of things in common—they all can eat plenty of chop and they love the country where they first tasted it."

Mike Robinson was stationed in Gbeapo Kaweaken, Grand Gedeh County, Grebo country, from 1975 to 1977. He worked as a forester with Bureau of Indian Affairs and U.S. Forest Service from 1978 to 1988. He now works in Hawaii as a natural resource management consultant, operating a business called "Resource Management." Clients include private landowners large and small, as well as county, state, and federal government agencies. He is married with three children and "living in the best place on Earth."

Dr. Phillip Robinson, DVM, is the Campus Veterinarian at the University of California and Secretary of the Society for the Renewal of Nature Conservation in Liberia. SRNCL is an international non-profit group established in 1992 to promote the restoration of the wildlife and national parks program in Liberia. He first worked in Liberia in 1968 as a wildlife ecology graduate student and traveled widely in both Liberia and Sierra Leone collecting information on the pygmy hippopotamus. Over the years he has returned to Liberia for various conservation projects, including the feasibility studies for the establishment of Sapo National Park, which was chartered in 1983. Along with other members of SRNCL, he developed projects for fieldwork and community development in relation to nature conservation. He is past chairman of the World Conservation Union's Hippo Specialist Group, which prioritizes conservation initiatives for these interesting African species.

Nancy Douglas Rodgers was a Peace Corps teacher in Gbarnga and then Butaw, Sinoe County, 1964-1966. She is a language arts resource teacher and an English as a Second Language teacher on St. Croix. Her cooking has become a mixture of Caribbean and Liberian styles. Nancy provided the drums and rice bag to illustrate this book as well as several of the prints by Betty Stull. Her Liberian students made the drums for her as a going away gift.

Betty Stull Schaffer was the wife of a medical missionary when she went to Liberia in 1959 with four children. She had two more children before leaving in 1974. They lived at Zorzor and later Phebe. Betty took her hobby as an artist with her to Liberia, where the landscapes and village scenes inspired her charcoal sketches and oil paintings. She is now married to William D. Schaffer and lives in Southampton, Mass.

William Siegmann served as a Peace Corps volunteer in Liberia, 1965-1969, as an instructor at the University of Liberia and at Cuttington College. Before retirement, he was curator of African art at the Brooklyn Museum and a visiting professor at Pratt Institute. He provided the factual information for the section called, "WHAT IS IT?"

John V. Singler, of New York City, taught at St. Joseph's School in Greenville, 1969-1970, the Episcopal High School in Robertsport , 1971-1975, and served as the organist at St. John's Church. A Fulbright Senior African Research Fellowship took him back to Monrovia in 1981 to study syntactic change in the Liberian English of Monrovia (Carried out in Lakpazee, which means "punch in the mouth," according to the linguists). His thesis for his master's from the School of Oriental and African Studies of the University was on Liberian language, philosophy, policy and practice; for UCLA, was on Klao (Kru) phonology and for his doctoral dissertation for UCLA was on variations in Liberian English syntax. He also collects and shares Liberian proverbs.

Roland Svensson (1910-2003), of Sweden, was commissioned by the LAMCO mining company to paint a series of watercolors during his stay in Liberia in 1969. The prints are a treasured keepsake collected by many people who lived in Liberia in the following decade. They depict life in two main areas, Buchanan, Bassa County, and Yakepa, Nimba County, where LAMCO iron ore mining operations flourished in the 1960s and 1970s. Roland generously allowed Friends of Liberia to reproduce his work as a fund-raiser for Liberian projects.

Joann Tweh worked as a Friends of Liberia intern in the summer of 1996, when she drew the sketch of the young refugee child. She left Liberia 1990 and obtained a bachelor's degree in German, spent some time in Germany and Austria, and then found her niche in the world of pharmacy. While she hasn't returned to Liberia since the war, her mother returns annually.

WHAT IS IT?

p. 1, 27, 81, & 107 These section dividers are computer scans of cloth made in Liberia. There are three major types of textile design used in Liberia. The first are designs created during weaving, generally the work of men who use a hand loom to weave long, continuous narrow strips of cloth. These are generally in a black and white striped pattern, although blue and white is also used. The second textile type is embroidered or appliquéd, also generally considered men's work. The third kind is pattern dyed. Pattern dying produces one-of-a-kind textiles. This is done by resist dying, painting, or stamping. Dying is woman's work and is regarded as a secret craft, handed down from mother to daughter, although others may be taught, usually for a fee.

p. vii Small intricately carved mortar given to Joan Keenan by a high school student she sponsored during the LEAP program in 2000.

p. xv Flat bags like this one are made of raffia palm fiber principally in the Loma and Kpelle areas, where the fiber is woven by men on a small loom. Another type of bag, commonly called a rice bag, is tubular and plated and woven by women to carry raw rice from the farm. Men plate bags in a tubular fashion to carry tools and weapons for hunting or farm work. The rice bag was the standard Peace Corps volunteer handbag in Liberia, as they were colorful, strong, and durable. When we went to Liberia in the late '90's for LEAP training, they were called "Peace Corps bags!"

p. 11 One of a pair of Liberian drums made by Nancy Douglas Rodgers' Sinoe County students in 1965 as a going away gift for her. They have survived two hurricanes and are still in good condition. Single headed drums like these, often called Sangba drums, maintain tension with a series of leather cords. The drum is beaten with the hands and generally has three tones that can be varied by the position of the hands on the drumhead. The head usually has three pitches—the lowest in the center of the head and the highest at the outer edge.

p. 12   A small woodcarving that symbolizes life, carved by Hansen of the Ganta Rehabilitation Center for Leprosy and Tuberculosis in Nimba county.

p. 19   The border for this and other pages is a scan of a "Kissi penny," an iron currency found among the Bandi and Loma as well. The iron was smelted locally and the coin was hand-wrought by the blacksmith. Originally used for trade, they are still used ritually on such occasions as the return of young men from bush school or for sacrifices and divinations.

p. 21   The cotton tree is among the largest tree species found in Liberia. It doesn't have commercial value as it has a soft wood texture. Cotton trees are commonly found in the vicinity of towns and villages where they are often spared from cutting. It is believed that they are the resting places of the spirits of departed elders. (The Pepperbird, Issue no. 2, 1995, p.1.)

p. 24, 34, & 54   Dan or Mano masks are usually used by male associations for rituals, education, social control, and entertainment purposes. They are thought to embody powerful spirit forces and are also as intermediaries between boys sequestered in bush school and their mothers in town. Their benign countenance serves as a calming influence.

p. 49   This Kpelle horn was purchased from a musical group that visited our house in Owensgrove during the 1966 Christmas season. These groups would play at different houses

160

in exchange for food, drink, or money. (This is much like on St. Croix during the Christmas season.) Four, and sometimes six wooden trumpets of different sizes are played as an ensemble in interlocking style. They are blown through a raised mouth piece on the side, much like that of a trumpet or trombone. The musicians traditionally perform to celebrate and announce the chiefs on formal occasions.

p. 50 The editor stands on a "monkey bridge" in the mid-'60s. These hanging bridges, made from strong liana vines woven together and hung from trees, are commonly found in northwest Liberia. Made in secret by the elders of the Kpelle tribe, these masterpieces of engineering are reputed to be built in a single night by the "country devil."

p. 71 This brass pendant mask was purchased in Liberia in the '60s, but it is actually from the Baule in the Ivory Coast and is simply used as jewelry.

p. 91 This is a small mask made of elephant bone basically in the Dan style for personal masks. It is a "passport mask," which is used as a protective amulet rather than as any actual entree to secret society as is widely believed.

p. 104 The mudskipper, periophthalmus barbarus, on this stamp is a fish that can breathe air. These fish are very active on land, often climbing the roots of mangrove. With their bulging eyes, they can see in all directions, but their eyes have become adapted for viewing things on land, and underwater images are blurred. (The Pepperbird, Issue no. 2, 1995, p. 7.)

ARTWORK

Roland Svensson

d'Azevedo, Kathy. *Kwi Style Cooking.* Pittsburgh, 1962.

Hultman, Tami (ed.). *The Africa News Cookbook, African Cooking for Western Kitchens.* New York: Viking Penguin, Inc., 1985.

Human Resources Project. *Come Let's Eat.* Peace Corps Liberia, 1975.

The International Women's Club of Liberia. *The Liberian Way of Cooking.* Monrovia: The Department of Information and Cultural Affairs, 1968.

Clarke, Clarice C. (ed.). *Native Recipes.* St. Croix: University of the Virgin Islands Cooperative Extension Service, 1994.

Phebe Hospital Auxiliary. *Phebe Cookbook.* Pipestone, Minn.: Nicollet Cookbooks, 1981.

Sandler, Bea. *The African Cookbook.* New York: Carol Publishing, 1994.

Wilson, Ellen Gibson. *A West African Cookbook.* New York: Avon Books, 1972.

d'Azevedo, Warren L. (ed.). *The Traditional Artist in African Societies.* Bloomington, Ind.: Indiana University Press, 1973.

Delange, Jacqueline. *The Art and Peoples of Black Africa.* New York: Dutton & Co. Inc., 1974.

Dendel, Esther Warner. *You Cannot Unsneeze a Sneeze and Other Tales From Liberia.* Niwot, Col.: University Press of Colorado, 1995.

Gay, John. *Red Dust on the Green Leaves.* Yarmouth, Me..: Intercultural Press, Inc., 1973.

Henries, Richard and Doris. *Liberia: The West African Republic.* London: Macmillan & Co. Ltd., 1966.

Humphrey, Sally. *Family in Liberia.* Minneapolis: Lerner Publications Company, 1987.

Johnson, Isaac. *The Leopard and the Deer, New Day.* Vol.14, No. 3 (Department of Education, Monrovia, May-June, 1967), 6.

Johnson, S. J. M. *Traditional History and Folklore of the Grebo Tribe.* Monrovia: Liberian Bureau of Folkways, 1957.

Korvah. Paul Degein. *The History of the Loma People.* Oakland: O Books, 1995.

Liberian Information Service. *Proverbs of Liberia: Vai, Gola, Grebo.* Monrovia: Liberian Information Service, 1963.

Miller, Randall M. (ed.). *Dear Master, Letters of a Slave Family.* Athens, Ga.: The University of Georgia Press, 1990.

Moore, Bai T. *Ebony Dust.* Liberia, 196?. Nelson, Harold D. (ed.). Liberia, a Country Study. Washington, DC: US Government Printing Office, 1985.

Nelson, Harold D. (ed.). *Liberia, a Country Study.* Washington, DC: US Government Printing Office, 1985.

The Pepperbird. Society for the Renewal of Nature Conservation in Liberia. San Diego, Calif.

Sullivan, Jo Mary. *Liberia in Pictures.* Minneapolis: Lerner Publications Co., 1988.

Warner, Esther. *New Song in a Strange Land.* Boston: Houghton Mifflin Co., 1948

167

HARVEST MOON

BY BAI T. MOORE

Of all the moons the gods bestowed
Glato* is the farmer's dream.
She brings the golden paddy fields
And drives the hungry moons away.
All the field, like a thousand incense burning
Fill the air with fragrance,
Of golden heads of rice
Of okra, corn and condiments
With which the farmer's spouse
Can keep aglow her hearth.
Along the winding village trails
Melodious harvest song in glee
From lips of carefree maidens,
Welcome love and merriment
When the harvest sun is setting
Over the hills, the trees and fields,
T he family moving to the town
Are silhouetted against the sky
With all their home utensils
Gently balanced on the head.
Glato is the planning moon
For feast to those who long have gone
To the fertile farming lands
Where all the tribes must someday meet;
It might have been the village doctor,
Gifted in the arts of cures,
Or the midwife of the village
Who rescued innocent maidens
Beset with fears of nature.

168

Or perhaps a lowly sire,
Who was sought in every council
And envied by some tyrant chief,
Or the jovial village smithy
Whose communal place of duty
Called the farmers from afar;
Or a village belle or lad
On whom the tribe bestowed
T he secret of their mores.
For these perhaps there'll be no cow,
But the farmer's only goat or sheep
Will grace the palate of the friends
Who come to share in mirth
T he memory of the ones departed
To the fertile farming lands.
In harvest moon when tom-toms
and the singing
Of the young entune the jungle
With a gripping syncopation,
And the moonbeams turn to silver
A hundred million silent leaves,
T he surging urge of dancing feet
Along the winding village trails
Beat up a rhythmic tempo.

*Glato is Dewoin word for October

WRITTEN IN 1952 TO CELEBRATE THE HARVEST IN THE AUTHOR'S
VILLAGE OF DIMEH.

FROM EBONY DUST, P. 42-43